BERNIE NICHOLLS

BERNIE NICHOLLS
FROM FLOODLIGHTS TO BRIGHT LIGHTS

Bernie Nicholls
with Ross McKeon and Kevin Allen

TRIUMPH
BOOKS

Library of Congress Cataloging in Publication Data available upon request.

This book is available in quantity at special discounts for your group or organization. For further information, contact:

Triumph Books LLC
814 North Franklin Street
Chicago, Illinois 60610
(312) 337-0747
www.triumphbooks.com

Printed in U.S.A.
ISBN: 978-1-62937-866-4
Design by Nord Compo
All photos courtesy of the author unless otherwise noted.

CONTENTS

FOREWORD

BEFORE MY TRADE TO L.A, I looked at Bernie Nicholls as hockey's version of "Broadway Joe" Namath.

Wearing those bright, shiny purple suits and driving to games in a sporty convertible gave everyone the impression he had a flamboyant personality.

That was the impression we had of Bernie since we didn't spend much time with players on other teams in those days.

But when I got to L.A., and we became very good friends, I learned his personality was almost completely opposite of his reputation. Bernie was quiet, sincere, and very humble. I gravitated to Bernie because he treated people with respect, he was good with kids and never stepped out of line with his teammates.

I knew Bernie could take a lot of pressure off me on the ice, and make life easier in the transition going from Edmonton to L.A. The Kings had finished 18th out of 21 teams, so I knew we had an uphill battle. And coming from a Stanley Cup champion, one thing I learned was you win with 20 guys, and you lose with 20 guys.

My goal was to make Bernie and Luc Robitaille extremely comfortable because I knew their contributions were going to lead to a great deal of success for the hockey club. That's basically what happened. Bernie scored 70 goals, Luc had 46, and in 1988–89 we went from being a bottom team to a top team.

We could sense the change from Day 1. We were going to compete hard every night and try to make it a new highway for the hockey club. It was a fun year because no one anticipated the club getting to that level.

For Bernie, it was a Hall of Fame year. Simple as that. We'd go into every game knowing Bernie was going to do something really special. You could see Bernie was genuinely excited to get to practice. He was genuinely excited to work on things, and he was genuinely excited to get to the next game. It was infectious for our hockey club.

Bernie and I had fun together. Early in the season, one of the first few games, my kids' school asked if I'd give an autographed hockey stick for charity. I was walking out of the arena with the stick and Bernie asked what I was doing. I don't know why but I said, "I don't think you know, Bernie, but I've done this my entire career. When I take my pre-game nap I sleep with my stick."

Bernie started taking his stick home after the next game and I never told him the truth until the end of the year. Once he scored 70 goals I started to think maybe I should be taking my stick home every game, too!

We had a lunch routine, too. In those days we'd leave the house at 7:30, get to the rink where there was coffee, practice from 10:30 to noon and by 12:30 we were starving. I'd say, "Bernie, I'm going next door to McDonald's, let's go!" We did that religiously. When something's working you don't try to fix it, right?

Just by chance the NHL All-Star Game that season was in Edmonton. It had been a real grinding season to that point, an emotional year with the trade to L.A. And it was really hard for me to go back and play in Edmonton. I never did get comfortable. I never loved it, never even liked it because people there were always so good to me.

It was an emotional three days so Bernie went to our owner, Bruce McNall, and asked if we could take his charter flight to Atlantic City for a day before rejoining our teammates in Boston. Bruce went for it, and it was a really nice break for us.

At that time Bernie was starting to get a lot more attention. There was a lot more pressure and things were building up for him that maybe he had never gone through before with so much media attention. Bernie handled it extremely well, and his mindset never wavered.

Bernie never changed while everyone around him was trying to figure out: Where did this guy who'd been in the league for a few years come from? And now he is going to score 75 goals maybe?

I think it was fun for Bernie. He took it all in, accepted the responsibilities, the challenges and just got better and better. Bernie and I spent a lot of time together just talking hockey and talking about life. He was the exact opposite of what people thought. He was very much concerned for teammates, loved life, and was close to his family.

The following season the hockey club came to me at midseason and said a deal to trade Bernie to the Rangers to improve our team was going to go down. And I remember asking, "Are you sure? This is a huge deal because Bernie has been a big part of the success of the team, not only within the group but the fans love him. Are you guys sure you're making the right decision?"

They called back the next day to have coffee, and it was right near the All-Star Game. I remember thinking this is so emotional and so uncomfortable. The one thing I never did in my career was tell management they needed to trade this guy or not trade that guy. It was never part of my makeup.

They sat me down and said to get to the next level we couldn't win with three or four guys. We needed to have a team. The Kings were getting two NHL caliber players—Tony Granato, who was going to be a mainstay on that penalty-killing unit and second line, and Tomas Sandström, who was a 40 to 50 goal scorer. The deal made sense even if the timing didn't. Bernie was going to a great organization, a great city, and a very good hockey club. It was emotional for everyone, but at the time the trade made sense for both organizations.

That's just the worst part of hockey. There's a lot of times I'd sit there and think, "Oh my gosh, it was so emotional when I got traded." But it's just part of the game. It's heart-wrenching for everyone, and that was definitely one of those times.

I tell Bernie all the time, you got to go to New York and, more importantly, you've got a rule named after you—The Bernie Nicholls rule. Now no one can get traded at the All-Star Game.

I do a lot of charity events and fantasy camps and Bernie is always a phone call away. He's always there to help anyone. People who attend enjoy the opportunity to play, but they really love to mingle and socialize with the players. They want to hear stories about playing, winning, and all that sort of stuff.

Bernie is exceptional at communicating with the fans and the players at my camp every year. He's always the first one there and last to leave. Bernie is a special man. He did a lot of great things for our game and he did a lot of great things for me personally.

—Wayne Gretzky

INTRODUCTION

MY WIFE THINKS BERNIE NICHOLLS is charming and engaging and she has never met him. Because this book project was completed during the Covid–19 pandemic, the interviews were all done on Zoom or speaker phone.

While Bernie and I talked about life in the NHL in the 1980s and 1990s, my wife would hear chunks and snippets of our conversation. It didn't take her long to formulate an opinion about who Bernie is and what he stands for.

"That's a player who truly loved the game and the people in it," she said. "When you listen to him tell his story, you can still hear the excitement in his voice about what it was like to play the game and what it was like to live a player's life. He seems thankful for the opportunity he had. You can tell he put his heart and soul into it."

That's what few people understood about Bernie when he played. Behind his pink suit, top hat, snakeskin boots, sports cars, and a golf cart with surround sound, there was an athlete who was as dedicated to his work as any master craftsman.

Some people viewed his usual carefree, joyful attitude as a sign that he wasn't working hard enough to be the best. But nothing could have been further from the truth.

You can be a guy who clowns around morning, noon, and night and still be a warrior when you are on a hockey rink. You can be a guy who can drink a chocolate milkshake while he stretches and still score four goals in a game.

His father, George Nicholls, taught him the value and honor that comes from perfecting the nuances of his sport. George spent hours in the family kitchen showing Bernie how to win faceoffs and he preached the importance of shot-blocking, penalty killing, and standing up for your teammates.

He believes in the sanctity of that work with religious conviction. In the best of ways, Bernie spent his entire career making sure his dad was proud of the way he played.

What George didn't have to teach Bernie was how to score goals because his son seemed to have a knack for doing that on his own. He is one of only eight players in NHL history to score 70 or more goals in a season.

Bernie is a small-town Canadian lad who discovered quickly that he liked to golf, play poker, bet the horses, and run with the celebrity crowd. But once he pulled on his equipment and laced up his skates, he was all business.

Coaches generally appreciated Bernie because they knew they would get a consistent level of play. Teammates liked him because he treated everyone with respect and pretty much liked everyone he ever played alongside.

Teammates also learned that Bernie could be happy-go-lucky most of the time and still play a hockey game as if his life depended on it. One of the constant themes in doing interviews for this book is hearing former teammates saying their perception of Nicholls' competitiveness changed after they played with him.

Despite registering a 150-point season, Nicholls might be one of the most underrated players in NHL history. He certainly is one of the most misunderstood players the NHL has ever known.

In this book, Bernie shows you what's behind his curtain. He explains, often with a comedic touch, what it was like to be a small-town boy playing in the NHL. He paints a colorful portrait of what it was like to be in the NHL in the 1980s and 1990s. Most of all, Nicholls provides a frank account of what he was thinking when he was playing alongside Wayne Gretzky, dating *Playboy* bunnies, and partying with celebrities like Jack Nicholson and Stevie Nicks. Hope you enjoy the read.

—Kevin Allen

CHAPTER 1

HOLLYWOOD HOCKEY

WHEN I ARRIVED IN SOUTHERN CALIFORNIA to play for the NHL's Los Angeles Kings in 1981–82, my story already read like a Hollywood script.

Small-town Canadian boy goes to the big city and discovers a world far more entertaining than he ever imagined. The only difference: my story was not a fictionalized account.

If you had written my tale as a screenplay before it occurred, it would have been rejected as implausible. One minute I am trapping and skinning beavers, muskrats, and otters with my dad in Northern Ontario and shooting my first deer at 15. The next minute I'm in Southern California, scoring goals in the NHL, partying with Academy Award–winning actor Jack Nicholson, beating Tiger Woods at golf, and dating a *Playboy* centerfold.

In my first full month in the NHL, I registered three hat tricks in a span of 10 days.

I had it all going on in my early years with the Kings. Driving a baby blue Corvette. Roller-skating near Manhattan Beach. Taking batting practice and shagging fly balls with the Los Angeles Dodgers. Eating sushi, roasted artichokes, and clams instead of meat and potatoes. When my parents came to visit, they wouldn't touch sushi. They couldn't believe I would eat raw fish. My life seemed alien to my friends and family back home.

My salary was $70,000, but I felt like a millionaire because two summers before I had been carrying heavy blocks and mixing cement to build the foundations of houses and buildings. My wage was $4.25 Canadian per hour. At the time, I told myself I would make sure I never had to work again. That turned out to be true.

I went from living in West Guilford, Ontario, population 70 (20 of them related to me), to living in the bustling Los Angeles area, which boasted almost 10 million residents. I grew up playing hockey on an outdoor rink called Tag Alder Gardens in West Guilford. It had natural ice, created by water pumped in from the Gull River. Fifty-watt light bulbs strung down the center of the rink kept it lit. I'd shovel off the snow and skate every night, no matter how cold it was.

Now I am playing hockey in Los Angeles where the average January temperature is in the high 60s and some days it's in the high 70s.

I had never flown on an airplane or been to the United States before I was drafted by the Kings.

Flying over the Great Western Forum as I descended into the Los Angeles International Airport for the first time, I saw the palm trees and the Hollywood racetrack and thought: *This so fucking cool!*

My favorite singer back then was Hank Williams Jr. My favorite song was "A Country Boy Can Survive." But I was thriving, not surviving, in Los Angeles. I was in love with the great outdoors and viewed myself as a hunter as much as a hockey player. My two goals in life were to play in the NHL and take down a moose.

The embarrassing truth is that I didn't know Los Angeles had a hockey team when the Kings drafted me. But it only took me a day or two in the Southern California sunshine to warm to the idea that I could love the West Coast as much as my former neck of the woods.

I would have time to bag the moose later.

By my second NHL season, I dressed like I had stepped out of the *Miami Vice* television show. I paid $1,800 for a pink silk suit. My wardrobe included Izod shirts, black and white boa constrictor boots, cowboy boots made from ostrich, and snakeskin shoes. I also wore a striped suit with a top hat. That was my gangster look.

Almost from the moment I set foot in Los Angeles I wanted the coolest and funkiest outfits. My suits were all custom tailored. Pricey high-end stuff. I don't know where I got that from. It wasn't my dad. I'm not sure he owned a suit.

My teammates' attitude was, *What the hell is he going to wear next?!*

I had one suit that looked like the sleeves were partially cut off. My wardrobe included some flowered vests.

Not everyone could pull off dressing the way I did. I was willing to try, and it worked out for me. Still today, when I see someone sharply dressed I stare at them. To me, clothes are fun. I feel good when I look good.

Sometimes I wore sneakers with my suits. Kings Hall of Famer Marcel Dionne was bothered immensely by that fashion statement. He thought the team should fine me for the sneakers, but that never happened.

When I landed in Southern California for the first time, I stayed in a hotel that was nine miles from the Culver City practice facility. It was a simple drive from the Marriott Hotel to the rink for my first practice. The Kings didn't want me going on the freeway. They wanted me to go under the freeway and through Culver City. That's not what I did. I ended up in Santa Monica, down by the beaches. I had no idea where I was or how to get back. This was before the introduction of cell phones and GPS. I stopped and asked for directions to the Culver City Ice Rink. But the people I approached had no clue Culver had an ice rink.

A drive that should have lasted 10 or 15 minutes ended up taking me more than two hours. That was my introduction to my new team. I was a no-show for my first practice.

I wasn't the first player to ever get lost driving in Los Angeles. But I seemed to have more crazy things happening to me than the others.

The truth is that I probably had to make a bigger adjustment off the ice than I did on the ice when I arrived in the NHL. People said I was cocky as a player, but it wasn't cockiness as much as I had scored in every league I played in. In 1978–79, I posted 40 goals in 50 games for the North York Rangers in Junior A hockey. In 1979–80, I registered 36 goals for the Kingston Canadians in the Ontario Hockey League. Then I followed that up with 63 goals in 65 games for the Canadians. In my first pro season, I managed 41 goals in 55 games for the New Haven Nighthawks.

I felt the Kings should have never sent me down. When I looked at our roster, I thought the only reason they demoted me was because I had a two-way contract. The other centers had one-way contracts. That meant the Kings would have to pay them NHL money to play in the American League. My salary was significantly reduced when I went to the AHL.

When I was finally called up, the only reason I didn't have early success was coach Parker MacDonald did not play me often.

My first NHL game was November 19, 1981, in the memorable Calgary Corral, where the boards seemed five feet high. We lost 6–3. During my first shift, I witnessed Kings defenseman Jerry Korab being rammed from behind into unforgiving boards. A Flames fan banged on the glass to get everyone's attention. When I arrived at his location, I saw some of Korab's teeth resting on the ledge of the boards.

Welcome to the NHL. I'd played one shift and I'd already seen a teammate's teeth knocked from his mouth.

MacDonald was old school and didn't trust younger players, or at least he didn't trust me. I didn't play many shifts. When we went to L.A., I dressed and didn't play a shift. It wasn't surprising when I was returned to the Nighthawks.

My break came when MacDonald resigned midseason and was replaced by Nighthawks coach Don Perry. He brought me up to the Kings with me, and he wasn't afraid to play me.

Goal scorers need confidence. They need to score to gain confidence. I went my first eight NHL games without scoring. My breakthrough came in my ninth game, March 9, 1982, when the Kings played the Colorado Rockies in Denver. With my former roommate Jay Wells in the penalty box for elbowing, I scored a breakaway short-handed goal at 5:35 of the first period. I deked goalie Glenn "Chico" Resch to beat him. I can document that because someone sent me a photograph of the play.

That goal removed the piano off my back. We won 2–0 and I netted both goals. Resch, a classy player, signed his goalie stick and had it sent over to me after the game.

It was important that my first goals were meaningful. What people never understood about me: winning was more important to me than anything else in sports. No matter what I was doing, I have always hated losing. When I was young, I would be mad if I lost to my mother in cribbage. I love to gamble, but it isn't about the money as much as it is about the winning. When I beat you in cards, I don't want your money as much as I want your pride. If we are both predicting the outcomes of NFL games, I will be mad if you get more right than I do.

Scoring two goals in a 2–0 win felt like a big win for me. Having my first goal be a short-handed effort was also meaningful.

That was all about my dad. He taught me to take pride in faceoffs, penalty killing, and making the plays that teams need to make to win. My first goal coming as a penalty killer probably made him proud, although he certainly didn't tell me that.

I was proud that Perry used me as a penalty killer as a rookie. He had a lot of confidence in me, and I think he thought I was the best centerman after Marcel Dionne. Although we weren't a winning team, we had great leadership. Most of the centers don't want to help you

7

because you are trying to take their job, but Charlie Simmer, Dave Taylor, and Mike Murphy looked after me.

Those two goals were the thrust I needed to propel me into my scoring orbit. I had a burr up my ass because they didn't keep me at the start of the season. That just made me more determined. I knew my own strengths: I could win faceoffs, kill penalties, and most importantly, I could score goals. The reason why I probably had lasted until the third round in the NHL draft is that scouts were troubled by my skating style. I was born pigeon-toed, my left foot slanting inward. I wore braces when I was two, but the foot is still angled.

"He's so knobby-kneed he looks as if he is going in two directions at once," former Kings coach Don Perry once said about me. "But it's not so much that he's a bad skater as he is a bad-looking skater. He actually has good balance, and he's moving along faster than he looks. But I don't care what he looks like as long as he can put the puck in the net."

Going up to the NHL, down to the minors, and then up again in my first professional season, it took nine games to score my first NHL goal. But once I got going, I was quite comfortable competing against NHL talent. I finished the season with 14 goals in my last 14 games. That included the feat of registering three hat tricks in a span of five games. Korab started calling me the "Mad Hatter."

I had 10 goals in those five games. My final numbers were 14 goals and 18 assists for 32 points in 22 games. I then opened the 1982–83 season with 16 goals in my first 17 games, giving me 30 goals in my first 39 games in the league.

What I remember most about that period of my career was feeling excited about being able to compete against the world's best players and doing it in a city where every day seemed like you were living in a movie.

Underscoring the fantasy aspect of my life was the day famed boxer Muhammad Ali showed up in our dressing room.

When I was leaving the Forum after practice, Ali was walking up the ramp next to me. He is shadow boxing me, bobbing his head, and jabbing at the air.

Are you fucking kidding me?

"You probably don't remember me, do you?" he asked.

"No, I don't," I said. "But my mum and dad went to Toronto once to watch you box, and they are going to love hearing this story."

I was thrilled. Muhammad Fucking Ali talking to me.

I was living a dream, although L.A. traffic was always a nightmare.

In my hometown, it takes roughly 40 seconds to drive between the two signs on Kennisis Lake Road that welcome you to West Guilford. My town is much smaller than Mayberry of *Andy Griffith* fame. Andy at least had a barber, doctor, and sheriff's office in his town. West Guilford had a garage/filling station, store, and restaurant. It was a 90 miles for us to drive from West Guilford to the nearest McDonald's. That's still true today.

Early in my career, I was given a rental car when my car was in the shop. It turned out the rental car had a faulty gas gauge. It registered full when it was empty. Of course, I discovered that while I was driving on Interstate 10 on the way to a home game.

There happened to be a major boxing event that night and I was already running late because traffic was creeping along. When the car coasted to a halt, I abandoned it and somehow managed to walk off the freeway without getting killed. I found a convenience store and offered a stranger $50 to drive me to the Forum.

I arrived at ten to seven for a 7:30 game, and the team was already on the ice for warmups. By the time I was dressed, the Kings had returned to the dressing room. Clearly unnerved by my escapade, I missed a wide-open net. I was a wreck. The whole evening was a nightmare.

The next day I called the rental car company about what happened, but when they went to reclaim the car it was nowhere to be found.

I've never recovered from my L.A. driving experience. Even today, if I find traffic somewhere I become a little jittery.

Young. Naive. Curious. All of those attributes made my life in L.A. an adventure.

In my first season, I lived with teammates Jay Wells and Daryl Evans in a four-bedroom El Segundo house overlooking the ocean. I was the only single guy. I remember I had borrowed Jay's car; I was driving it home after a game, and it had no gas. He told me I had to put gas in it, and I had $20 in my pocket.

I pulled into a gas station and a hooker jumped in my car. I'd never seen one before. I'm from West Guilford! We didn't have hookers. I said, "All I got is $20."

The next morning I said to Jay, "You need gas."

I'm experiencing L.A. for the first time. I'm 20 years old. Who cares what you do when you're that young?

I was literally living in the fast lane. I probably led the NHL in speeding tickets. By the mid-1980s, I had my license suspended and then revoked.

One night, I got stopped in the desert going 110 miles per hour. I saw the lights in my rearview mirror, but I thought, *There is no chance in hell they are catching me!*

But when the lights drew closer, I realized the car trailing me wasn't out for a Sunday drive.

Another night, a female police officer nailed me for 95 in a 55 mile per hour zone. She was at Kings' practice the next day and told me she had to give me a ticket because one of her superiors was in the cruiser with her.

Another time, I was clocked at 85 in a 35. That required a court appearance. The judge knew who I was and said, "Do your speeding on the ice."

All of my speeding tickets came in a Corvette I was driving. I bought a Ford pickup truck with big tires. I don't think it would go 70 miles per hour. My hope was the truck would slow me down.

My life, both on the ice and away from the rink, was like an adult fairy tale. It seemed like one day my father was teaching me how to win faceoffs in our kitchen and the next day I'm sitting at the Forum Club next to Morgan Fairchild.

She was wearing full-length lynx fur. I owned a full-length otter coat, but I never wore it in California. I'm not sure Morgan knew who I was or was interested in what I had to say. But the fact that I was talking to her reminded me that my life was a fantasy.

I never met Hugh Hefner, but I went to the Playboy Mansion. I also dated one *Playboy* Playmate and hung out with another. Lorraine was an April 1981 Playmate and she asked me to go to a Fleetwood Mac concert.

We ended up backstage to meet up with Stevie Nicks. Then Lorraine, Stevie, and I went out on the town.

I dated a 1980 *Playboy* Bunny—Lisa Welch—for a while. Nobody would have believed me, except I brought her back to Canada with me. Somewhere in that time period I also dated a Los Angeles Lakers cheerleader.

It was a crazy time for me. After many games, I'd stop at the Forum Club. You could never guess what might happen if you stopped there.

I wasn't the only member of the Kings with an active social life. We also had the Press Club and that's where the owners, management, and coaches hung out after the game. My coach, Pat Quinn, told me one time that he walked into the Press Lounge one day and he found team owner Jerry Buss stretched out on the couch and making out with a young woman.

When I played for the Kings, every day was an adventure. The Los Angeles Dodgers invited me down to Dodger Stadium. They let me shag fly balls, take infield practice and batting practice. I cranked a couple out of the park. But what I really remember was running into the outfield wall chasing a fly ball. I still have the jersey they gave me.

From the first day I pulled on a sweater, I loved being an NHL player and everything that went with that. People would criticize me for laughing and having fun on the ice, but I couldn't help it. I just loved everything about the game.

I wasn't trying to be a different kind of NHL player. That's just who I am. When it comes to hockey and life, I am engaged. I like to enjoy myself. As soon as I got into the NHL, people started talking about my goal celebration.

When I scored a goal, I lifted my knee waist high and pumped my right arm a few times. I started doing that when I was seven because I love scoring goals. I took my profession seriously, but I have fun playing this game.

Former NHL player Kevin Dineen once called me the "craziest guy in the world who never drinks" in an article in the *Los Angeles Times*.

That was the truth. I was always the life of the party, but I didn't drink alcohol. I tried a couple of times, but it wasn't for me. I don't even enjoy the taste of beer. Teammates would ask me about it, but no one ever gave me a hard time about it. It wasn't like I was staying in my hotel room and not hanging out with the guys.

Partying was part of my lifestyle. I went to the Playboy Mansion, sat courtside at Los Angeles Lakers games, and spent more than my fair share of time at the racetrack. My dad had taken me to the Woodbine Racetrack in Toronto when I was a young, and I had developed a taste for betting the horses long before I came to L.A.

I stayed out as late as anyone, but I was drinking Cokes instead of beers. That created a small problem because the drinkers would go home and sleep like babies. I'd be wired from drinking all of that caffeine. I had trouble sleeping. At least I wasn't hungover.

Several New York Islanders players, particularly Clark Gillies and Bryan Trottier, have told the story about when I was a young NHLer: I came into the Islanders' dressing room after their morning skate at the Forum and asked players to autograph a stick. NHL players just didn't do that. At worst, they might ask their trainer or equipment guy to get it done. But that's not what I did.

I wish I could tell you that I stood in the hallway and waited for them to come out. But that's not what happened. Trottier and Clark Gillies both recall I came into their room, asked them for a stick, and went around to each player to get it signed. I was like a 10-year-old child, saying, "Can I have your autograph please?"

Seven hours later, I was going to battle the Islanders.

I heard a similar tale about Gretzky meeting Guy Lafleur. Gretz was 18 and scheduled to play in the Montreal Forum for the first time. The trainer led him around the corner and there's Guy smoking a dart and holding a beer. Gretz got to meet him. I was similar that way; I just wanted to meet my heroes.

But I think my Islanders introduction showed I felt like a kid when I played the game. That hasn't changed. Even today, when I pull on my equipment to go out on the ice, I still feel like a kid.

It didn't take long for me to earn a reputation as a colorful player. I was called up to the Kings for good on February 18, 1982, and in November of 1982, nine months after my arrival, *Sports Illustrated* published an article by the late Jack Falla highlighting the uniqueness of my on-ice success and off-ice personality.

"Bernie has more self-confidence than anybody in the world," my roommate Jay Wells told Falla.

Falla wrote that my goal-scoring celebration was "the most flamboyant post-goal routine seen in L.A. since the days of Eddie Shack's choppy-strided Night Train runs across the Forum ice."

At the time the story appeared, I was second in the league in goals with 16 in the first 17 games.

Sports Illustrated didn't write much about hockey. To be featured in the national magazine in my second season was an indication of the impact I was making. But *Sports Illustrated* acclaim came with a jinx. At least that's what people said. When you were featured in the magazine, bad things happened to you. Sure enough, I went down with a knee injury right after the article was published. Red Wings defenseman Willie Huber sent me crashing into the boards and I suffered a partially torn knee ligament.

After I recovered, I wore a bulky knee brace. I struggled to adjust to it. After my memorable start, I scored only 12 goals in my last 54 games to finish with 28 for the season.

Off the ice, I was fully exploring what Southern California had to offer. I attended every Lakers game, hanging out with Magic Johnson, golfing every chance I could, dating many different women, and betting on horses at Santa Anita and Hollywood Park.

Jockeys Sandy Hawley and Chris McCarron worked as off-ice officials in the Forum penalty box and I got to know them well enough to pick up racing tips.

"How does tomorrow look?" I would ask while I was waiting for my penalty time to expire.

"I think it looks all right," McCarron would say.

I'd ask how his card looked the next day and he would tell me if he liked his horses or not.

Hawley was one of the best jockeys from Canada and McCarron was probably one of the top three in the world. I was well known enough to walk into the jockey room and McCarron would tell me what he thought about the horses running that day.

I had a friend who was also a jockey, although he was not as successful as McCarron and Hawley. He would win one race a month, and McCarron might win three in a night.

If this friend saw me at the racetrack, he would stand up in his saddle if he liked his horse. It was like a third-base coach signaling the batter. He ended up getting mixed up in drugs, though.

The Kings started to worry that I was headed in the wrong direction. Coach Don Perry, general manager George Maguire, and the team's head of security, Lou McClary, staged an intervention.

I was surprised by how much information the Kings had about my lifestyle. They knew about who I was hanging with, about the women I dated, and what I was doing with my spare time. They believed I had a lifestyle that could go sideways. I don't think they knew that I didn't drink. I told them that I was in the middle of that world, except I didn't drink or do drugs.

But I was into women and going to the track. My thought was that two out of four wasn't bad. Plus, I was being reasonable with my betting. I understood there was potential to find trouble: I like to go to the track. I like to bet. I like to gamble. But I don't bet or play cards with money I can't afford to lose. At least I had that going for me.

The other important factor was that there was nothing more important to me than being an NHL player. I would never jeopardize that.

The Kings' intervention didn't anger me. I thought, *Wow these guys really care about me!* I understood they were protecting one of their team assets, but they also were looking out for my best interest.

I think they believed me when I told them that I wasn't involved in drinking and drugs and wasn't making crazy bets. I was mostly making $20 bets, and occasionally laying a $100 bet on a good tip.

But I took our meeting to heart, and by the following season I had a place of my own.

I never shared the details of that meeting with my parents, even though calling home was a daily ritual. I always loved talking to my mother because she was always positive. To her, I never played poorly. We could lose 6–1, and if I scored the lone goal, she would say, "Oh, you played good tonight, honey."

God bless her. Until the day she died, my mother believed I never had a bad game. Whenever I needed a pep talk, or a shot of confidence, I could call Mum. I could be in the worst slump of my life, and she would say, "You're playing great."

If it was a close game she couldn't watch. She'd go into the bedroom and be yelling out to Dad, "What just happened? What are they doing?"

"Why don't you get out here and watch, for Christ sakes?" my dad would shout.

My dad wouldn't say much. He didn't have to. I always knew what he was thinking. If I wasn't playing well, he'd tell me to work harder and keep my chin up. He was never going to tell how well I was playing, but I know he knew. Sometimes he would tell me to shoot more, which was his way of saying he didn't have much faith in my wings. I could tell he was proud of me.

I didn't tell my parents that the Kings had sat me down to discuss how I was living my life. My dad knew I was playing the horses; we'd talk about how I was doing. And they knew I was seeing various women.

But they didn't worry about it the way the Kings did. They trusted me because they knew who I was. They had raised me. They knew my values. My dad especially knew that hockey came first with me. All of my abilities, I owed to his instruction. When I was learning the game as a youngster, he was my coach. To share your success with your parents is the best thing about being an NHL player. It meant the world to me that they found so much enjoyment in my career. As soon as the Kings televised games on Prime Ticket, I bought my parents a satellite dish to watch my games. Even though half of my games started at 10:30 PM eastern standard time, my dad and my mom wouldn't miss any.

I had so much fun playing for the Kings in the 1980s, even though they didn't know what to make of me. I know coach Pat Quinn liked me, but he had a hard time accepting that I liked to have fun as a player. I just couldn't be as serious as he wanted me to be.

One time, we were in a team meeting and I was just chewing gum and listening to what he had to say. Apparently, I was smiling, which is pretty normal for me. If we are talking about hockey, I'm enjoying it.

But Quinn couldn't take the smile.

"Wipe that smile off your face or I'm going to wipe it off for you," Pat said in anger.

I was stunned. I meant no disrespect. Pat reminded me of my father and I had nothing but respect for my father. I wanted to please Pat. But that's when I kind of understood that it was going to be challenging sometimes just to be myself.

CHAPTER 2

PRANKS FOR
THE MEMORIES

DAVE "TIGER" WILLIAMS was my linemate for a season in Los Angeles. He was a fellow bowhunter. We got along famously most of the time.

But he wanted to kill me more than once. That's not an exaggeration.

I always believed that being an NHL player should be fun on and off the ice. That meant I was the clubhouse leader in pranks. They were all intended to be fun. The usual reaction was the victim taking an oath to reign revenge down upon me. But not everyone loved my pranks. My linemate Dave "Tiger" Williams, one of the NHL's toughest players, didn't appreciate a couple of my efforts.

He brought a box of books he had written into the dressing room because he had been asked to give them to children at a birthday party. The kids were going to skate at our practice facility at Culver City. I thought it would be funny if I gave all of his books to guys on the team to take home to their children. When he came back to his dressing stall and discovered half of his books were missing, he became enraged.

When Williams was interviewed about the incident for this book, he remembered thinking, *I'm going to teach that little bastard a lesson, and he'll never do it again.*

Williams added, "I thought about what I could do to scare the shit out of [you]. I knew I can't kill or hurt [you] because that wouldn't go over very well."

Coincidentally, I had started bowhunting and had brought my bow in to show Tiger. An experienced bowhunter, Tiger was going to give me some pointers.

Instead, Williams nocked an arrow, and pointed in my direction. I was at the end of our long, narrow dressing room.

"Pumper-Nicholl Bernie?" Tiger yelled. "You just messed with the wrong guy. Now stand up, you bastard, I'm going to kill you!"

I hit the floor as the arrow flew a couple of feet over my head. Defenseman Al Tuer was lacing up his skates when the drama started. The arrow traveled 20 yards and lodged in an air conditioning vent less than a foot from Tuer's head.

My memory was that the room went silent. But Tiger remembered players saying, "Don't kill him, Tiger, don't kill him. We'll give you back your books."

Tiger yelled at me, "Stand up, you bastard, I'm not going to shoot you while you're laying down!"

I didn't move, not even a muscle twitch. Neither did any of my teammates. Tiger fired a second arrow and yelled, "Don't ever mess with me again!"

Tiger finished dressing and headed out on the ice to wait for his teammates. Not many went out to join him.

Somebody told coach Pat Quinn what happened because he went on the ice to talk to Tiger.

"Hey, how ya doing? Are you okay?" Quinn asked Tiger.

"Great," Tiger said.

"Well, we've got a problem," Quinn said. "Your teammates don't want to come out here today. They're not sure what your state of mind is today."

The situation did blow over, but Williams recalls many of the players' wives were angry over the incident.

"Some of my teammates were pretty pissed off," Williams said.

That wasn't the only time Tiger became enraged by one of my practical jokes. It's common practice for players to leave tickets for their wives, girlfriends, friends, parents, etc. I knew Tiger was leaving tickets for his wife, Brenda.

Stopping by the box office, I left a note for Brenda that read: "I want to thank you for what happened in the bathroom after the last game."

Tiger was straight as an arrow. He would never do anything like that. Tiger undoubtedly had some explaining to do. Apparently, Brenda was upset. She didn't see the humor in my prank. Apparently, he wasn't sure initially who had done this to him.

Before practice, Quinn stopped me. "I don't know what you did, but I know it was you," Quinn said. "And Tiger Williams is going to kill you."

I apologized to Tiger and then his wife. I could tell by what Pat said that he believed it was time for me to stop pranking Tiger.

It was no secret that I loved a good prank. If something funny happened to someone, I was often the first person to blame. Teammates. Coaches. Trainers? No one was safe. I didn't look to embarrass people or pull mean pranks. I was just out for a good laugh. But as my career went on, I had to look over my shoulder often.

Tiger wasn't the only person to wish harm upon me because of a prank.

My favorite stunt was hiding behind the shower curtain in someone's room on the road and waiting to surprise them. I'd go to the front desk and ask for a key. Back then you didn't even need to show identification. They'd give a key to almost anyone, especially if you told them your teammate lost his key. I'd know the room and who the roommate was in case I had to answer questions the front desk might have.

The best time to get someone was right after the team meal following a morning skate. I made sure I arrived at the room first. I would hide behind the shower curtain. I'd grab a pillow for protection in case someone started beating the shit out of me. Then I'd just wait.

I made sure I didn't make any noise after the door to the room opened. It usually didn't take long for my victim to enter the bathroom. The first thing a guy does after eating is go to the bathroom. In most of the hotels, bathrooms are small. The shower curtain was right next to the toilet.

I'd wait until they'd get good and comfortable.

Man, I got Marcel Dionne real good one time. He came in, had no clue I was hiding in there, and sat himself on the toilet. I came out from behind the curtain yelling, "AHHHHHHHHHHH!" and Marcel jumped sideways. He flew off that toilet flat on the floor! And he had a bad groin, too.

Fell flat on his ass!

"You're friggin' nuts, I swear," he would say.

I nailed defenseman Scott Stevens, too, at the 1985 World Championships in Prague. He was a big, tough defenseman. But he ran out of the bathroom straight into the bedroom naked and started screaming on top of the bed. We had a good long laugh after that one!

Another one: John-Paul Kelly was probably the biggest guy I played with early in my career. He weighed about 225 pounds. When I finally opened the curtain and yelled he started screaming on the toilet!

Kelly was so surprised he was clenching his fist and I could see the veins popping out because he didn't have a shirt on.

I enjoyed scaring people. Even if I got scared, I would laugh about it. To me it's just fun like that. I know no one else did it. It was easy to get them. After a while everyone is kind of on to it. It would have been pretty cool if we had cell phones back in the day. It'd be hilarious to get someone on the toilet while he was on the phone.

Most of them knew right away it was a joke, and that it was me. They'd eventually get a good laugh. But always my victims' first reaction was to just lose their minds.

When I put shaving cream in my former Kings teammate Brian MacLellan's bed, under the covers, he started punching me, mostly in jest. MacLellan became general manager of the Washington Capitals.

Maybe the best prank ever was when I got our trainer Pete Demers. He's legendary in Los Angeles. He holds the record for 2,632 consecutive games as an athletic trainer. Amazing. Great guy, too.

I remember we were in the Embassy Suites in New Jersey, and I pulled the hide-in-the-shower prank to perfection. Once he was settled into the bathroom and started to brush his teeth, I sprang out from behind the curtain screaming. Demers ran out, jumped on his bed, and started kicking his feet up and screaming like a kid. I scared him badly. Real bad.

"I'll get you.... It might not be today. It might not be tomorrow. It might be next week, next month, or next season. You might go to another team, but I'm going to get you!"

Demers admitted later that he was terrified.

"I thought I was going to have a heart attack," he said. "As a U.S. Air Force veteran, I'd had a terrifying experience while serving, and I'm really easily frightened and surprised ever since."

And if he didn't try to get me back on the very next trip! Lucky for me, I had the habit of pulling the sheets and covers loose from the bed because I didn't like to sleep with them tight. I hate that feeling. So I barely have any covers on me when I sleep. Every hotel I go to, I rip down the sides and throw the sheets up just so they're not tucked in.

Well, *someone* got into my room, pulled the sheets back and took the biggest dump right there on the sheet! Then that someone re-made the bed as if nothing happened. If I hadn't pulled all the sheets up first and tucked my feet in there? Oh my God.

For years, Pete would never admit what he did. Instead, he'd tease me, "I'm still looking for that guy, I'm still trying to help you find who did that. Because that's not right."

Yeah, it was payback for me getting him because I got him good!

Did anyone ever get me? Not often, but they sure tried! One time with the Kings we were doing a shoe check on the rookies. Mark Hardy and I were trying to get this young kid. I was seated at the table and talking to the kid sitting next to me. Out of the corner of my eye I saw Mark coming through under the table.

Mark got back out from under and gave me the nod. That was my queue to tap my glass with the fork and say, "Shoe check!" Everybody looked at their shoes to see if someone had smeared them with ketchup, mayo, mustard, ranch dressing, or whatever else was available. The kid beside me looked down and didn't say anything.

I asked, "Bud, did you check?" He said he was good. So I looked down, and Mark got me!

The worst shoe-check prank I ever did was against former Kings teammate Dean Kennedy. He had a pair of suede cowboy boots. I put ketchup or some other substance all over them. I felt bad about that one because I ruined them. In my defense, it's dark under the table and you don't know what kind of footwear you are smearing stuff on.

One prank I attempted at a Kings training camp in Victoria, British Columbia, did backfire on me. I had a couple of French Canadian rookies in the room next to mine. With the help of teammate Phil Sykes, my plan was to go out on my balcony and then jump onto their balcony in the middle of the night. Then I was going to enter their room and scare the hell out of them.

I didn't care that we were on the fifth floor and that we had to make about a four-foot leap to go from one balcony to the next.

The balcony jump went fine. What didn't go fine was the prank. When we jumped in the room and screamed, we didn't find the Kings' rookies.

Unbeknownst to us, they had moved out and a forty-ish woman and her mum were staying in that room.

Sensing the trouble we were in, Phil and I hustled through the door and made the reverse balcony leap. I couldn't get out of the room fast enough. They must have thought we were both Batman.

Police were called. Coach Pat Quinn was summoned. It was presumed that it was a prank. Quinn professed ignorance about who might have done it.

At practice the next day, Quinn just kept skating us around and didn't blow the whistle. Finally, he called me over and I told him the sordid tale. He told me we had indeed terrified "two elderly women." We paid for their rooms and that was the end of it.

You obviously don't prank guys on the ice or during a game. You'll chirp an opponent or say something personal to get them off their game. Everyone is looking for an edge. No one said you can't try to goad someone into doing something.

Before we later became teammates with the Kings, Marty McSorley and I were rivals when he played for Edmonton. Marty got more out of his talent than anyone I know. That's not a knock on Marty. His eyes and hockey sense were as good as anybody. Obviously Gretz loved him. That's why he brought him to L.A.

It was pretty easy to get Marty going. We were playing the Oilers and a whistle stopped play in front of the net as someone was getting a penalty. The referee skated toward the penalty box and Marty started giving me a face wash in front of the net. Big guys do that to the smaller guys at times.

There was only one referee, and he was preoccupied talking to an off-ice official at center. So, without him looking, I turned and punched Marty as hard as I could right between the eyes. I just drilled him. Then

I skated as fast as I could, stood beside the referee, and said, "He's coming! He's coming!"

Marty came and speared me right in front of the referee. And he was sent to the penalty box. It worked!

Marty's version of this story is slightly different from mine. "[You weren't] standing next to the ref," Marty said. "[You were] trying to hide behind him."

His description of the spear is "not super hard, but hard enough."

"I felt the ref would know that Bernie did something," Marty said. "All he did was give me a major and he didn't give Bernie anything. I vividly remember Bernie saying, 'Here he comes! He's going to get me!' And that was a time when you could get someone later. But Bernie didn't care. He was cocky enough, arrogant enough, and maybe even tough enough to not care."

Off the ice, Marty is the sweetest guy you'll ever meet. In the dressing room, though, you have to be careful. He loves gross pranks. Let's just say, don't ever go in the shower with Marty.

Marty was tough on the ice, that's for sure. I know he stuck up for me a number of times.

My reputation as a prankster gets me in trouble sometimes when it deserves it. Demers believes I was the culprit who dropped water balloons off the roof of a hotel and onto the heads of Kings coaches and players when they were coming back from a road dinner.

One of the balloons apparently dinged our late coach Pat Quinn.

Demers believes Quinn is waiting in heaven to exact his revenge. "He now knows who did it," Demers says.

I can tell you it wasn't me. First, I respected Pat too much. Second, I would have been afraid of what he might do to me.

Even though I'm long retired from hockey, the pranking continues. When we were at the hunting cabin, I placed a rubber snake in a cooler. I've scared the fuck out of people. People run off screaming.

When I was a kid, I liked being scared. Someone would get me and then I would laugh about it. I think it's fun.

Just recently, I may have hid in the shower when my girlfriend was going in there and scared the hell out of her. The look in her eyes when I jumped out of shower can't be described.

CHAPTER 3

BROKEN BONES AND BONUSES

IN 1983–84, THE ALL-STAR BREAK was in my jaw. I had been named to play in my first All-Star Game. But in the game before, in Calgary, defenseman Paul Baxter created the fracture with an elbow to my face.

But we didn't know that until a few days later.

After the incident, I went to the bench, not feeling great. But I took my next shift and the one after that. That's when I was drilled into the boards and my jaw popped out of joint. Today, as I ponder how many concussions I've had, I wonder if I had one or two that night.

After the game, I couldn't close my mouth. Still didn't feel well. But the doctors believed I was all right.

With their blessing, I traveled to New Jersey to play in the All-Star Game. I couldn't eat the night before the game. But I played in the game, not registering a single point in the Campbell Conference's 7–6 loss.

As soon as I returned to Los Angeles, the orthodontist told me the jaw was broken. He wired it shut. When I was told I couldn't play the next game, I cut the wires. My jaw popped out of joint again. I had to have it rewired. I left the wires alone the second time.

All I could eat was Klondike bars, mashed potatoes, and milkshakes. But they let me play with my mouth wired shut. I started out between 175 and 180 pounds and I lost 19 in five weeks.

You feel weak. Your breath stinks. It is a miserable experience.

I remember getting peanuts from the flight attendant on a trip to Edmonton. I had one tooth in the back of my mouth. That's where I shoved in the peanuts. By the time I had three or four peanuts in there I couldn't swallow them. We hit turbulence and now I couldn't get water because no one could leave their seat. I sat there for an hour with a mouth full of peanuts.

While I was wired shut, I recall doing something stupid in a game in Buffalo. It required big Larry Playfair to respond.

"I'll break your fucking jaw again if you keep doing what you're doing," Playfair said.

I ran out of patience with the wires. I was supposed to wear them for six weeks. But after five weeks, when we were in St. Louis I cut the wires.

As much as I was loving my life as an NHL player, it wasn't always sunshine and manicured fairways. The NHL is a tough, violent league. I liked to hit and that meant that players were going to target me.

I took pride in trying to stay in the lineup through injuries. I only missed two games over the four seasons from 1983–84 to 1986–87. In the season I broke my jaw I scored 41 goals and registered 95 points.

My 1984–85 season was even better. It was Pat Quinn's first season behind the bench. I loved him as a coach. We got along extremely well. Under his command, I had my first 100-point season.

On November 13, 1984, I also had my first four-goal game and established a new record by scoring one goal in each period, plus a fourth in overtime.

I was the first to do that. Since then, Sergei Fedorov, Alexander Ovechkin, and Mika Zibanejad have done it.

I scored 13 seconds after the opening faceoff to start. The second one gave us a 3–2 lead in the second period. I had a power play goal three minutes into the third to tie it, 4–4. And the fourth one came on a power play three minutes into OT to win it.

Quebec had a good team that year. They had two of the Šťastný brothers—Anton and Marián—and the Nordiques also had Michel Goulet. It's a shame Quebec lost its franchise. They sold out all the time.

More importantly, they had the best hot dogs of any arena! The hot dog bun was toasted. Guys would eat those delicious dogs before the game.

I received a bonus for scoring 100 points. I can't remember if it was $25,000 or $50,000—or maybe even $100,000! I was a young kid, but we all went crazy over the 100th point. Most of the guys knew about the bonus so everyone got excited.

The 100th point came on an assist midway through the third period of our last game. I had a bonus for 30 goals, 40 goals, and probably 50, which I didn't get.

And a bonus for 90 and 100 points.

Thinking about my bonuses reminds me of a time later in my career when I was playing for the Rangers and Dino Ciccarelli was with Washington. He had a bonus for 40 goals and we were playing them the last game of the season. There was a faceoff in my end and I whispered to Dino, "Just get behind the centerman."

I let the faceoff man win the draw clean back to Dino, but he didn't score. I tried to help him out! The game didn't mean anything. I thought it was an all right thing to do.

Back to the 1984–85 season. I had a 25-game scoring streak that started halfway through October and ended in a mid-December game against the Oilers. Pat Quinn played the hell out of me that night, and even called timeout with a couple minutes to go with us up 7–2. We're beating them pretty bad, and for him to call a timeout? Well, you'd never do that. He did it to rest me. He wanted me to be at my best for my last shifts to extend the streak. The Oilers would do that to rest Gretz.

During that 1984–85 season, the Oilers lost only three playoff games and won their second straight Stanley Cup. The Smythe Division was always entertaining to say the least. It was always enjoyable to play division games against Winnipeg, Calgary, Edmonton, and Vancouver. You knew it was going to be wide-open hockey. It seemed as if the scores were always 7–6 or 8–5. Compare the Smythe Division to the Patrick where all their games were 3–2 and 2–1. Such a big difference. Our division was a lot more fun to play in, and you knew where you had to go to get anywhere. It was through Edmonton.

Just days after we were eliminated, I found myself in Prague to play for Team Canada in the 1985 Men's World Championships.

It was the only time in my pro career I played in an international event. If you're available for the tournament that means your team is out of the playoffs. That's bad. But the opportunity to play for my country was unbelievable. That's good. What's funny is I took nine suits with me because I didn't know any better. I figured I'm going over to play a bunch of games. I would need suits. Instead, I get there and am handed matching team sweats. We didn't even wear suits. Boy, that was dumb of me. I took a whole bunch of shit I didn't use! I roomed with Stevie Yzerman, who was 19, four years younger than me. I always liked the guys I played against, the big skill guys like that. To get to know him and room with him, I got really close to him. That was Mario Lemieux's first year, and he was 19, too. It was a talented roster—Rick Vaive, Larry Murphy, Ron Francis, Kevin Dineen, and Dave Taylor.

We received the silver medal after the host Czechs beat us, 5–3, in the gold medal game. To advance to that contest, we beat the Soviet Union 3–1. It was the first time Canada beat the Soviets after 11 straight losses, dating to 1977.

Russia's goalie was Vladislav Tretiak, who I got to know later in Chicago. But he was injured and didn't play in the tourney. The backup was Vladimir Myshkin, who lost to the Americans in the "Miracle on Ice" game in the 1980 Olympics. The Russians and the U.S. played for the bronze medal, and they had a big brawl on the ice as tensions still ran high five years later. The Russians won 10–3. The experience was awesome. Being away with different guys. The city itself was beautiful.

I remember they had to fly me first to New York because I had to get my passport to go on. Why did I need a passport? I grew up in West Guilford. I wasn't flying anywhere.

And I remember they'd pick three guys after each game to pee in a bottle and get drug tested. The food was a little suspect. In the hotel where we stayed, the bar was off limits to anyone not staying there. But they allowed the hookers in. If you were a guest, you were not allowed in there.

No one else other than the girls, which was fine for some of the guys. I'm pretty sure they didn't mind! It was the first time I wore the Canada sweater. I never played at the World Junior Championship.

What a great thrill, and to play with guys I played against in the NHL. To have the opportunity to play with Mario was memorable. You think someone that big in the game wouldn't come over, but he did and represented his country with us. He led our team with six goals and 10 points in nine games. I'd hear the Canadian anthem in the NHL, but when you're representing your country it's different. You see it all the time with the emotion on their faces—and it's no different if you're in Canada or the U.S. When your anthem is playing it's pretty special. Every athlete loves that. I didn't have a great tourney—no goals and two assists in 10 games. I saved my jersey, got the silver medal, and I've got great memories. A lot of guys don't get that opportunity because their NHL teams are successful every year.

That was my only chance to play in a big international tournament because the NHL didn't start participating in the Winter Olympics until my final year in San Jose. By then, I was 36 years old. It would have been hard, even in my prime, to make Canada's roster with all the talent the country had at the center ice position. Playing for my country reminded me of how much I'd miss home. I called my mum pretty much every day.

The next season, 1985–86, I don't know what happened. We had a bad year and finished last in the Smythe. Marcel Dionne, Dave Taylor, and I had pretty good seasons. I led the team in points with 97. Marcel was next with 94 and Dave had 71. Everybody else was down in the 40s or lower. Tiger Williams (49) and Jimmy Fox (31) played with me. We didn't have enough depth. It was just a bad year. Two of the Kings' big prospects—Jimmy Carson and Luc Robitaille—made the team in 1986–87. The Kings took Jimmy second overall a couple months before, and Luc jumped up after getting picked in the ninth round in '84. We had a lot more balance than the year before. Luc led the team with 84 points, I had 81, and Jimmy—just 18 years old—had 79 points. Marcel had 74 points before he was traded to the Rangers. And we lost to Edmonton in the first round.

As much as I loved playing in Los Angeles, it wasn't always fun and games. As previously mentioned, I hate to lose at anything, and the Kings lost often in the 1980s.

In my first seven seasons in Los Angeles, we never finished higher than fourth in our division. We won only 36 percent of our games in that period and won one playoff series. And we call that the "Miracle on Manchester." No one believed we would beat the Wayne Gretzky-led Oilers in my rookie season.

I took losses home with me, and I was often miserable. I was up half the night. After I married, the situation wasn't good.

Losing just wears on you. Everyone just hates to lose. It was Pat Quinn who told me to do whatever you want after the game. Don't sulk. Have some fun. The minute you leave the dressing room the game is gone. Don't take it with you. Then come back the next day and come back to work.

That was the best advice I ever received. When I went back to work for the Kings as a power play coach in 2012, I told the kids just let it go. That is important. You can't take it home with you, which I did for years. The sooner you can let that go the better. I think that's why you see guys out there, maybe having a drink with their families. Well, you know what? It's okay. The game is done.

You can't do anything about it now. You move on. The worst move you can make as an athlete is to take a loss home to your family. It took me time to understand that. What's the two- or three-year-old kid thinking? *Dad is always mad! Why is he yelling at me?*

Once you leave the arena, you have to let it go. Especially a playoff series. Golfers talk about that concept of having a short memory. If you double bogey a hole, you can't be thinking about that on the next hole or you may hook a drive.

The last thing you want to do in an NHL playoff series is stay up all night and think about what happened. It's not good for your family or for your mental approach to the next game.

Every athlete will tell you they will remember all their losses. I played in the New York Rangers–New Jersey series that went seven games in 1994, and I think that was the greatest series ever played. And I played in the seven-game series when the Kings beat Oilers in 1989. I scored two goals and had two assists in the last game when we won.

But I have more detailed memories about the loss my New Jersey Devils suffered to the Rangers than the Kings' win where I played well.

And the losses did get to me in Los Angeles. One season, 1985–86, we were 23–49–8. That was ugly. We won 28.7 percent of our games. That means we were winning just over once every four games.

But I had more optimism about our future when Bruce McNall arrived on the scene in 1986. He bought 25 percent of the team originally, became the primary stockholder in 1987, and, in March of 1988, bought the rest of Jerry Buss' shares.

McNall had made his fortune in rare coins, and you could tell immediately he was a mover and shaker. He loved being in the sports world. McNall was a promoter at heart, the guy who invites you into the tent to see the greatest show on earth.

I remember Buss brought him around to meet the guys. He was fun to be around. He's one of those guys you like instantly, a jolly old guy, always happy. We quickly became friends. We went to the famed Palm

Restaurant in Los Angeles. Back then, it still had pictures of celebrities on the wall. He and I started going to the racetrack together. We were buddies.

McNall believed the Kings could have a larger profile in Los Angeles if we could start contending for the Stanley Cup. He wanted to bring in some big-name players and make it happen.

Robitaille and Carson played impressively well in 1987–88. Carson scored 55 goals and Robitaille had 53. I had 32 goals and 78 points in 65 games. I missed games because Doug Gilmour broke my index finger with a slash in November. The team let me go home to Canada while I was recovering. I got to hunt with my dad. We made the playoffs but lost to Calgary in five games in the first round. Former Kings player Mike Murphy, a great guy, took over behind the bench the second half of the previous season. He played the hell out of me, too. But he got fired halfway through '87–88. It wasn't his fault, and it wasn't fair. You can't fire 25 guys. The team just didn't play well. Robbie Ftorek succeeded Murphy.

It was the same old Kings. And then McNall delivered on his promise to turn this franchise around. He did it in a very big way. McNall brought in the greatest player in NHL history. And no one saw it coming.

CHAPTER 4

BERNIE AND WAYNE'S EXCELLENT ADVENTURE

ONE WARM SUNDAY IN AUGUST 1988, I was at the Genesis Celebrity Golf Tournament in Massachusetts when a teenager I just met dropped news on me that landed like a bombshell.

The kid had been drafted eighth overall by the Chicago Blackhawks two months before. You could tell he was outgoing and overflowing with confidence. His name was Jeremy Roenick. As soon as we were introduced, Roenick blurted out, "I hear Wayne Gretzky is getting traded to the L.A. Kings."

Boom.

His words were a two-megaton news blast.

"Are you fucking kidding me?" I asked, stunned by what he had said.

Roenick was not fucking kidding. He was sure of his information. Even though he hadn't played a single game in the NHL, he knew what was going on there. Mike Eruzione, hero of the 1980 American Olympic gold medal triumph at Lake Placid, had invited me to this tournament. He knew Roenick and said I could trust the information.

I didn't know what to think because I was close to owner Bruce McNall and he hadn't uttered a word about trying to acquire Gretzky. Roenick's scoop was a shock.

But I wanted to believe it was true. Acquiring the NHL's greatest player did sound like something McNall would do. McNall made his fortune speculating on the rising value of ancient coins, and now he was going to acquire the rarest treasure in the sport of hockey. This move fit the way he did business and lived his life.

I knew I had to call Bruce immediately. As soon as he picked up the receiver, I told him what I had heard about the Kings' acquiring Gretzky.

"Did that really happen?" I asked.

He giggled. Anyone who knows McNall knows what that means. McNall giggles when he can't contain his excitement.

"What do you think about that?" McNall asked, telling me what I wanted to know without actually confirming the deal had occurred.

The trade was announced August 9, and the Kings gave up young star Jimmy Carson, former first round pick Martin Gélinas, three first-round draft picks (1989, 1991, and 1993) and $15 million for Gretzky and two hard-nosed forwards: Marty McSorley and Mike Krushelnyski.

Carson had scored 92 goals over his first two seasons in the NHL. But with all due respect to Carson's ability, it didn't matter who we had to give up. We were getting a player who was probably bigger than the game he played. Many Americans couldn't name an NHL team, but knew Gretzky was the sport's greatest player.

Before the Gretzky trade, the Kings didn't draw well. The only time we'd see a big crowd in L.A. would be if Gretzky and the Oilers came to town. That's why I knew it would be a circus with Gretzky now wearing a Kings jersey. I couldn't wait for that to happen.

At the time of the deal, Gretzky was 27, in the prime of his career, coming off a 149-point season and his third Stanley Cup championship. He was only 27 months removed from registering a 215-point season.

Some Californians didn't know hockey, but they got the idea of what was happening when the Gretzky deal was said to be similar to the Boston Red Sox trading Babe Ruth to the New York Yankees.

Before Gretzky's arrival, one reporter covered the Kings on the road. In September 1988, when we went to training camp in Victoria, British Columbia, we had 10 reporters milling about.

In 1988–89, Kings tickets were the hottest tickets in Southern California. Of course, the price doubled. Some long-time season ticket holders were priced out of the lower bowl. They had to move higher. Once the regular season started, Kings mania was nuts. Players were often the lowest profile celebrities in our dressing room. Kurt Russell, Goldie Hawn, Tom Hanks, Michael J. Fox, Sylvester Stallone, and Kevin Costner were just a few of the folks we saw on a regular basis. Magic Johnson didn't regularly attend our games, but we started seeing him in our dressing room once Gretzky was there.

The late John Candy was there often because he was a close friend of both Gretzky and McNall. The three of them got into some business together, including the purchase of the Toronto Argonauts in the Canadian Football League.

It was a circus at every game as people made a pilgrimage to see the Great One. Gretzky was already popular before the deal, but he was rebranded by the trade. Everyone wanted to see him in a Kings jersey.

I immediately became Gretzky's guy. Everywhere he went on the road, he took me with him. I wasn't sure why it had happened, but I was happy about it. I asked players in Edmonton whether Gretzky had one guy there, and they told me no.

Maybe Wayne saw my potential and wanted to help me reach it. Before games, he'd tap me on the pads and say, "I need you tonight."

Or maybe he just liked hanging with me.

I remember in New York we went to restaurants, backroom parties, card games, and saw Mafia people all because I was with Gretz. We had it all. The people he knew, and who wanted to meet Gretz.... I was just his shadow. I was there with him and got to experience it all. And you'd experience it at his level. They were talking to Gretz, they weren't talking to me. But you could see what it was like to be him for a day.

We mostly hung out on the road. But Wayne started asking me to have lunch with him after practice. When it occurred the first time, I assumed we'd drive off to dine at a quality restaurant. That's what we did on the road.

But that's not what Wayne had in mind. We'd stroll up to the McDonald's and grab a quarter-pounder and shoot the shit about the league, sports, or golf. It's fun to talk sports with Wayne because he knew league statistics by heart. He not only knew what was happening at the top of the scoring race, but he knew what was happening in the seventh, eighth, and ninth spots. He knew who had scored three goals or registered points the night before. He knew the standings and schedules of every team in our division. He also knew what was happening in other sports.

Rogie Vachon was our general manager, and McNall treated him well. But player moves started at the top with Bruce. He also talked to Wayne every day. That made perfect sense to me because Wayne was well versed on what was happening everywhere in the league. If I owned a team with the greatest player ever to play the game on it, I'd be running shit by him, too.

We acquired goalie Kelly Hrudey that season, and he played well. I started to believe we had a shot to win it all. The excitement surrounding our team also suggested that. As the season wore on, the Gretzky impact on the team, Southern California, and the NHL grew daily.

When we were playing a game in Hartford, the Nevada–Las Vegas basketball team coached by Jerry Tarkanian was in town to play a college game. The players asked to meet Wayne. Tarkanian came with them.

"When five of my players all want to meet a white hockey star, the guy must be pretty special," Tarkanian said.

It was as if the sports world was just discovering Wayne, even though he had been in the NHL for nine seasons. It was as if Gretzky were being rebranded. Everyone wanted to meet him, especially in Canada. It was tough getting in and out of places without creating a commotion. When the movie *Major League* debuted in 1989, Gretz and I snuck into the movie theater in Edmonton. But even in a darkened theater, someone spotted us. We had 50 people waiting for us when we exited the theater.

Gretz was kind to people. He wanted to sign for everyone. But you had to watch out because if he got started, he'd get mauled. We tried to help him out. We'd get him in and get him out. When we would go into a restaurant or bar, we would try to get into a back corner and then form a human barricade to prevent people from getting to him while he was trying to eat or have a conversation with a teammate.

Later in my career, I hung around several times with Michael Jordan, and he employed a bodyguard, a former police officer who carried a gun.

The situation with Wayne never got that bad, but if the Gretzky phenomenon had happened today he might have needed a bodyguard.

My time with Gretzky in Los Angeles was the best period of my career. Every day there was a new story to tell about what was happening with our team. The number of celebrities visiting Gretzky was so high that it was sometimes difficult to keep track of who was in the room, particularly after games. Our dressing room was frequently chaotic.

When we were playing in Vancouver, Gretzky mentioned that Canadian music legend Bryan Adams was coming to the game that night and was going to stop by the dressing room.

"I'd really love to meet him," I told Gretzky.

"No problem," he said.

That night after the game, I kept an eye peeled for Adams. I was near Wayne and there was a steady stream of visitors, some of whom Wayne introduced me to. I couldn't tell you who they were because I was focused on meeting Adams.

It didn't happen. We were dressed and leaving when I said to Gretzky, "I fucking thought you were going to introduce me to Bryan Adams?"

"I fucking did introduce you to Bryan Adams," Gretzky said. "I said, 'Bernie, this is Bryan; Bryan this is Bernie Nicholls.'"

"You mean that little guy was Bryan Adams?" I asked.

I don't know what I expected Bryan Adams to look like, but apparently it wasn't the guy Wayne introduced me to. Some nights we needed a program to sort out the celebrities in our room.

Life with Wayne was always entertaining. One night, we were playing in Pittsburgh and the Mario Lemieux versus Wayne Gretzky rivalry was a made-for-media event. In the 1987–88 season, Lemieux posted 168 points and Wayne had 149. In 1988–89, Lemieux had his best season with 199 points. The sports pages were full of the suggestion that Lemieux was now the king.

When we took the ice for the pregame warmup, I noticed a sign in the crowd that read: "This is Mario Country: Wayne Who?"

I'm sure Wayne saw the sign as well.

In the first five minutes of the game, we were killing a penalty together. Wayne scored a short-handed goal, after a pass from me. Exactly one minute later, he scored another. Again, I drew the assist. He had his hat trick by the 1:40 mark of the second period. By the time that period was over, Wayne had set me up for a pair of goals, giving him five points in the first 40 minutes.

When we came out for the start of the third period, I noticed the Mario Country sign had disappeared.

I did what I could to keep Wayne amused. One night, a bunch of us jumped in a taxi in Washington D.C. I was in the front seat. Wayne was in the back. I don't recall who else was with us. What I do remember is that I started to talk to the cab driver about hockey.

Those were the days when hockey wasn't as popular as it is today. TV coverage was lacking. Some people knew the big names, like Gretzky.

The cabbie asked if we were hockey players and told us he liked hockey. Then he started talking about Gretz.

"What do you think about that Gretzky guy?" he asked.

That was my opening. I chose my words carefully.

"He's just a wuss," I said. "He's overrated!"

I was laying it on thick. I couldn't see Wayne, but I'm sure he was stifling laughter in the back seat and smiling ear to ear. The poor cabbie just kept listening to me dump on Wayne.

Maybe he was hoping for a bigger tip. He immediately started to agree with me.

"Yeah," he said. "You know what? Now that I think about it, I don't think he's as good as people say. He's out on the ice all the time. He gets all the playing time. He must be selfish."

His rant continued for another minute until we reached our destination.

"Bud, the guy in the back is going to pay," I said. "It's Wayne Gretzky."

The poor cabbie didn't know what to do. He was looking, and in his mind he must have been going, "Holy shit," because he really was a hockey fan. He was embarrassed and we were amused.

Gretzky said about the memory, "The cab driver almost had a heart attack when Bernie pointed at me."

About my practical jokes, Gretzky said, "Bernie loved to prank, but I think we were together too much for him to bother with me."

Gretzky was a god in every NHL city. He always ate at five-star restaurants. Those restaurant owners wanted Gretzky in their restaurants. It was usually just Wayne and me. But sometimes we had a group, like the time we went to Studio 54 in New York City.

We hadn't been there long when we were told that Elton John was there and wanted to meet Wayne. Everywhere we went, someone requested an audience. Wayne always had time for everyone. But people had to come to him. He didn't go to them. That wasn't arrogance. That was just how Wayne did it. If you asked to meet him, he expected you to come to him. He may have been excited to meet other celebrities, but he always showed the same polite, cordial interview no matter who you were. He was just as cordial to an autograph seeker as he was to Elton John or Michael Jordan.

What I remember from the Elton John encounter was an interaction between one of Elton's people and Kings tough guy Jay Miller.

Miller asked the guy what he did.

"I'm Elton's bodyguard," he said, proudly. "I look after my guy."

"How much do you make?" Miller asked.

"Fifty thousand," he said.

Miller nodded.

"What do you do?" the bodyguard asked.

"I'm kind of like a bodyguard," Miller said, laughing. "I protect Wayne Gretzky."

"How much do you make?" the bodyguard asked.

"Two hundred thousand," Miller said.

The bodyguard's eyes grew as big as serving plates. I'm guessing the British chap didn't understand the nuances of being an NHL tough guy.

While the Gretzky show continued, we were also engaged in the serious business of transforming the Kings into a Stanley Cup contender. Before Gretzky's arrival, the Kings had won one playoff round in the previous 11 seasons and never advanced to the conference finals in the playoffs. In 1987–88, the Kings had finished 12 games below .500. The objective was to win it all in 1988–89.

McNall didn't just bring in Gretz to sell tickets and spark national hockey, which he did, but also to win.

When we won our first four games, averaging 6.5 goals per game, the hype grew even larger. We were 15–7 by Thanksgiving. I had 28 goals in those first 22 games. Gretzky had 17 goals.

We were not without controversy. In a game at Detroit in November, Gretzky slammed his stick on our net after we gave up a late second period goal against the Red Wings. We had rookie Mark Fitzpatrick in net and had a 5–0 lead at the time. Gretzky was just showing his frustration for having contributed a mistake that led to Fitzpatrick losing his shutout. He felt bad for Fitzpatrick.

The players didn't think anything about Wayne's display. How many times have you seen a player do that? Many. It has become a normal reaction to giving up a bad goal. But between periods, we started to hear that our coach Robbie Ftorek had told Gretz he was benching him.

Gretz was none too pleased. The coaches' room was next to the visiting dressing room at Detroit's Joe Louis Arena and we could hear a heated exchange between Ftorek and Gretzky.

"Twenty thousand people didn't come here to see you coach," Gretzky said at one point.

Yes, he did go there.

Playing in Detroit wasn't like playing in other NHL cities. Detroit is less than a three-hour drive from Gretzky's hometown of Brantford, Ontario. Many family and friends were there to see him play. Based on the cheering, I think half of Canada was at that game. It does feel like you are playing in Canada when you are in Detroit.

Ftorek was our no-nonsense coach. He had been a tough, hard-nosed, gritty, feisty—even a dirty—NHL player. He was unwavering in his convictions about how the game should be played and believed even superstars should be held accountable for acts that weren't to his liking.

None of us could understand how Ftorek could do that to a guy like Wayne who tried to do the right thing every day of his life.

No one in that arena had come to see Ftorek coach. But when the period started, Wayne was on the bench. At one point, Mike Krushelnyski turned around and said, "Robbie, you have to start playing Wayne."

It was an embarrassing situation. Eventually, Robbie started putting Wayne on the ice. But none of this escaped McNall's attention. Our next game was scheduled for Calgary and I was told McNall was coming to Calgary to fire Robbie.

But Wayne asked McNall not to fire Ftorek. Wayne didn't want someone to lose his job because he had a disagreement with him. That wasn't who Gretzky was. He didn't want to be the superstar who got someone sacked.

Unfortunately for the Kings, the media didn't let the story go. The *Hockey News* published a story with a headline: "The Pros and Cons of Robbie Ftorek."

The media made fun of Ftorek when he would say that he looked at Wayne as just one of his 20 players.

An editorial cartoon in the *Hockey News* cast Ftorek as one of the wise men gathered around baby Jesus in a nativity scene, saying "Well, as far I'm concerned, he's just another baby."

The *Washington Post* wrote a lengthy story in January outlining what they were referring to as a "feud" between Wayne and Ftorek. That's not what it was, really.

Wayne just wanted the whole thing dropped because that's who he is. He didn't want it being a distraction to the team.

McNall often said that people shouldn't look for any hidden meaning in Robbie's actions.

"Don't look too hard for the real Robbie Ftorek," McNall said in the *Washington Post* article. "The real Robbie Ftorek is the one standing right in front of you."

The bigger issue for our team was finding the right linemates for Wayne. When the trade was announced, I assumed Wayne would play with Luc Robitaille and Dave Taylor.

The previous season, Carson had played with Luc and Dave. I played with Jimmy Fox. We had a revolving door at the left wing. It didn't matter to me. I was just hoping to earn some power play time alongside Wayne.

But it was determined quickly that Robitaille and Taylor weren't right for Gretzky. Paul Fenton, Bob Kudelski, Mike Krushelnyski, Hubie McDonough, and Tim Tookey were among the players who got time on Gretzky's line.

According to an April 1989 issue of *Sports Illustrated*, one of the jokes making the rounds in hockey circles was that if you were the New Haven farm club's player of the week, "your prize would be a round-trip airfare to L.A., a trip to Disneyland, and a week playing on Gretzky's line."

Meanwhile, I ended up playing with Robitaille and Taylor. I felt as if I won the lottery.

Sometimes, Ftorek would use me on a line with Gretzky. I'd play center, and Gretzky would play wing. But it was understood that when we switched lines, Gretzky came on the ice first, and I would be second.

In the defensive zone, I played down low and Gretzky played up top. In the offensive zone, Wayne would set up where he always set up.

I didn't think it was difficult to play with Wayne. You only have one mission: get open. If you did that, Wayne was going to get you the puck. Don't ever tell yourself that Wayne can't make this pass because he can always make the pass. Expect the unexpected.

It's funny to me when coaches pull out the white board during a timeout and start drawing up a play. This isn't like football where you can draw up routes for all of us. Just put your best five players out there and let them improvise. Let them read what's available to them. In hockey, you just have to take what they give you. Wayne and I created many great plays together, but never did we know what we were going to do before we did it.

But I can tell you that playing with Gretz was my career highlight.

McNall was almost as popular as Gretzky. He was a colorful personality, and fans appreciated how aggressively he tried to improve the team. As soon as Bruce bought the Kings, he and I hit it off. I'm not sure why, although the explanation may have been as simple as we had similar hobbies. Bruce liked golfing, horse racing, and having a good time.

Hanging out with McNall was often surreal. Twice, I flew with him on a helicopter to go golfing in San Diego.

It was like being a character in a video game. We raced up the coastline, not all that far above the Pacific Ocean, weaving through downtown and then finally landing on a cul-de-sac in my Friendly Hills Estate neighborhood. McNall kicked my ass out of the copter and then his pilot whirled off to wherever McNall was headed. In case you were wondering, landing a copter in a residential area is absolutely illegal.

McNall liked playing the role of high roller almost as much as owning the team. He had so many Hollywood connections, and he enjoyed using those connections to help his friends.

Kind-hearted Bruce just couldn't do enough for his friends. One time, Wayne and I went to the horse races with Bruce in Calgary. Wayne and I had a tip on a horse to win. Many others must have received the same tip because the odds on our horse were low. He became one of the favorites. Bruce decided to help us by betting a bundle on another horse. As expected, the board quickly showed better odds on our horse.

Only one problem: our horse didn't win. Of course you can guess what happened. Bruce's horse won the race, and he received a big payoff. Wayne and I had so much fun hanging out with McNall. And often it was John Candy completing our foursome. Candy was such a loveable, jovial guy. He was always entertaining. He loved to golf. Believe it not, he had a decent golf swing. Because he was heavy, he didn't golf as well as he wanted to. But he always had a good time.

I remember talking to him about his role in the movie *Planes, Trains and Automobiles.* One thing led to another, and soon I was saying Steve Martin's lines and Candy was saying his lines right on cue. It was just as much fun as watching the movie.

McNall liked to hand out gifts to us. Once, he gave me two tickets to the Oscars. He gave me gold coins that were valued at $35,000 when I eventually sold them. He also gave me shares in three racehorses.

Another time, he called me into his office and handed me the keys to a 1989 green Jaguar convertible. As I recall, it was in celebration of my 50th goal that season. He gave Gretzky a black Jaguar. The final aspect of that story is that Gretzky had numerous mechanical issues with his Jag and mine ran like a dream.

In 1988–89, the Kings had four players named to the All-Star: Gretzky, me, Steve Duchesne, and Luc Robitaille.

Because the game was in Edmonton, McNall flew us up on his private plane. After the game, we were to fly to Boston for our next game.

Gretzky had a better plan.

He encouraged me to go ask McNall to fly us to Atlantic City, instead of direct to Boston, to give us a day off. Other Kings players received time off because of the All-Star break, but we had not. The problem with the Atlantic City plan was that coach Robbie Ftorek had scheduled a practice for Sunday night.

When I mentioned Atlantic City to Bruce, he thought it was a grand idea. He laughed and then called Ftorek.

"We are having trouble with the plane so the boys won't be in until Monday," Bruce told Ftorek over the phone.

What was Ftorek going to say?

While our teammates were practicing, we were at the blackjack table. Bruce pulled out his wad and handed each of us about a thousand dollars to bet.

Everything with Bruce seemed surreal. One time, he asked me to play with some corporate sponsors in San Diego. I flew down the night before and played. The next morning, I was standing in San Diego at 9:00 AM and I got to L.A. in time for a 10:30 practice. Bruce flew me on his private plane. It felt like the flight lasted 12 minutes.

Bruce had a limo pick me up at the airport and take me right to the arena.

I would not have changed anything about the time I spent playing with Gretzky. I loved hanging out with him. We had the perfect marriage. We never argued...unless you count the times after I'd miss an empty net after Wayne had set me up.

"Bernie, what happened?" Wayne would say when we returned to the bench.

"Wayne, I don't know," I would say.

I didn't ever want to let Wayne down. I've never met a better team player than Wayne. Some superstars are selfish. Every game is about them. Wayne was the exact opposite. What he wanted most was for all his teammates to have success.

Playing with Wayne was inspirational. If I scored a goal, Wayne would always say, "We need another one." If I had three points, he wanted me to get four. He said that because that was always his mindset.

Before playing with Wayne, I would think when you got a three- or four-goal lead, you shut it down and start thinking about the next game.

Wayne never thought like that. If we had four goals, he wanted us to score six. After we had them down, he wanted us to stomp on their throats. He was so driven. That's why he had those monster seasons. If he had four points, he wanted five. Once he had five, he'd work hard for six.

On December 1, 1988, I had the game of my life, registering a Kings' record eight points in a 9–3 win against the Toronto Maple Leafs.

I ended up with two goals and six primary assists. Every time I'd get a point, Wayne would whisper, "You got to get another one."

I had six points by the end of the second period, and it felt like I had a chance to match Darryl Sittler's NHL record of 10 points in a game, established on February 7, 1976.

I really felt like I should have scored six goals that night. That's how well I was playing.

When the 1988–89 season was over, Ftorek was fired. I was disappointed. I had no problem with Robbie. As McNall would say, "Robbie is Robbie." I never had an issue with him. He gave me plenty of ice time.

The new coach was Tom Webster. I didn't know it at the time, but he would end up being the only coach I didn't get along with.

CHAPTER 5

BROKEN PROMISE

WHEN I STARTED THINKING ABOUT buying a $1 million home near my Friendly Hills Country Club in Whittier, the person I wanted to talk to was not a realtor, a mortgage broker, or a tax expert.

The man I wanted to speak to was McNall.

McNall listened intently as I explained the home's features.

"I think it's a perfect investment," McNall said, and then added, "I'll never trade you."

That's all I needed to hear. I didn't want to buy an expensive house and then end up playing elsewhere. That's one of the worries of a professional athlete.

McNall treated me so generously that I knew I could trust him. He wouldn't purposely lie to me.

Not long before that conversation, I had negotiated—if you can call it that—a new five-year contract worth $750,000 per season. It was probably one of the simplest contract negotiations in NHL history.

McNall told me I didn't need an agent because he planned to give me whatever I thought was fair. I fired my agent Bill Watters and we met in West Hollywood. He asked me what I wanted. We talked and agreed on the years and $750,000. Honestly, if I had asked for $850,000, I believe Bruce would have given it to me.

Kings general manager Rogie Vachon didn't know I'd reached an agreement with Bruce. Not wanting Rogie to feel slighted, Bruce told me to just tell Rogie that I wanted $700,000.

"He'll come back to me and I'll agree to it," Bruce told me.

I called Rogie and we talked. I told him what I wanted: $700,000 for five seasons. It was so funny. He said, "Bruce will never go for that. There's no chance."

"That's what I want," I said, "and I deserve that."

Two hours later Rogie called back and said, "I went to war for you. I battled him. He didn't want to do it. And I talked him into it. I got the deal for you."

I was laughing in my mind. I couldn't believe he was taking credit for getting me the five year deal worth $3.5 million.

There was no specific reason why I asked Bruce for assurance that I wouldn't be traded, just a worry that it could happen. I don't think anyone expected me to score 70 goals again in 1989–90, but I was still having a strong season. I was on pace for 131 points. That was an average of 1.60 points per game, not too far behind my 1.89 points per game 1988–89 average.

But under new coach Tom Webster, the Kings weren't doing quite as well in 1989–90. The team was hovering around .500 midseason. And Wayne still didn't have the right wingers.

Meanwhile, Webster didn't seem to appreciate my contributions as much as Ftorek did. Either right before or right after Christmas we played a game and afterward, he announced that we would have the next day off.

However, he told everybody to ride the stationary bikes before they went home. We only had three older model bikes located outside the locker room. The bikes that had the strap around the wheel. They were terrible. I was one of the stars in the last game, and after I did some interviews and stuff, it was late. I just went home.

Two days later I showed up for practice and knew immediately Webster had a burr up his ass.

"Did you ride the bike before you went home?" he asked, already knowing the answer.

"I haven't rode a bike in nine fuckin' years," I answered. "Why would I ride one now?"

Obviously, he was pissed off by my reply.

The bike story worked its way around the NHL. After I was traded, Don Cherry referenced it on *Hockey Night in Canada*. "Somebody in L.A. should ride a bike off a cliff," Cherry said.

Trade rumors had been following me for a couple of seasons. That's why I asked McNall about it before I bought my house.

Rumors started again in January of that season, especially during a span when the Kings only managed a tie over one seven-game span. We dropped into fourth place in the Smythe Division.

McNall had promised a "big change."

Even before then, the media had speculated either Luc Robitaille or I would be traded. I even joked about it with Luc, asking him if he was going to start packing his bags.

Those rumors were the buzz at the NHL All-Star Game in Pittsburgh. Reporters had asked me about it at the press availability. Based on my conversation with McNall, l didn't think it would happen.

But it did happen.

On Saturday of All-Star weekend, Calgary Flames goalie Mike Vernon told me he heard that I had been traded to the New York Rangers. I was stunned to say the least and immediately tried to find Bruce.

Later that evening, he told me to come up to his suite. I was told I was dealt to the Rangers for Tomas Sandström and Tony Granato. I was put on the phone with GM Rogie Vachon.

I think Rogie felt bad.

I don't think Webster had anything to do with me being traded. He really didn't have any power. Nothing happened on the Kings without McNall signing off on it after talking to Wayne.

In looking at the big picture, I know I was traded because the Kings needed someone to play with Gretz. Robitaille and Taylor just couldn't play with him. Gretzky came from Edmonton where he had Jari Kurri, Paul Coffey, Mark Messier and now he's in L.A., still the greatest player in the game, with nobody to play with. It's too bad Luc couldn't play with him. He could have scored 100 goals.

McNall and Gretzky both felt bad about it.

"I had to weigh my own personal feelings," McNall told the *Los Angeles Times* about the trade. "But as the owner, I have to take away the emotional feelings and consider what is best for the team. I hate doing it. There are great things about being the owner of a team. Wonderful things. But there are also some bad things like this."

"I have to weigh what 16,000 people (a full house at the Forum) want," he added. "The thing is to win. The second has to do with individual players. This could be an unpopular decision. A lot of people are not going to like it."

Bruce felt bad enough that he bought back the shares in the racehorses he had given me for $45,000.

Vachon told the *Times* the trade had nothing to do with how I was playing.

"Bernie has been great for us," Vachon said. "This trade has nothing to do with Bernie Nicholls. The team is playing bad and we had to make a drastic change. If he was a bad player, we couldn't get two good players for him. He's a professional. I'm not ever going to say anything bad about Bernie."

I was beat up that season, dealing with an ankle and knee injury. But I was still producing. At the time of the trade, I had 75 points in 47 games, good enough for third in the scoring race behind Mario Lemieux and Gretz.

The Rangers wanted me—that's the way I decided to view the trade. It wasn't like I was being traded for a case of beer and three dozen pucks. In 1988–89, when I was scoring 70 goals, Granato had scored 36. Sandström had 32. He had scored 40 two seasons before. And Sandström was miserable to play against. He was one of those guys who did what he needed to do to be successful. He could be a dirty SOB. The story came out that the trade talks really turned serious when the Kings said they wouldn't make the deal unless Granato was included. Originally, the Rangers had offered Ulf Dahlén and Sandström.

Sandström and Granato were both 25 years old, and they seemed like they would be a good fit for Gretzky.

McNall, Gretzky, and Vachon thought they were doing something positive for the Kings, but I told Vachon that night, "I think you are getting the raw end of the deal."

The Rangers wanted me because they were having their own issues. Talks started after the Rangers went through a 1–11–3 skid.

It was a strange All-Star Game. Later that night, after the meeting with the Kings, I ended up at a press conference announcing the deal. I pulled on a Rangers sweater for the photographers. It was all such a blur.

A reporter asked me how I wanted to be introduced before the game, and I said, "As a Ranger because that's what I am."

As luck would have it, the Rangers were scheduled to take a three-game western road swing to Edmonton, Calgary, and then Los Angeles. I'm sure the Kings were cursing their bad luck. I had played in L.A. for nine years and I had a large following. Many Kings fans didn't like the deal.

When I came out for the warmup, there were plenty of signs: "Trade Rogie," read one. "We love Bernie," read another. Several implored the Kings to bring me back. I had only been gone a week.

The game couldn't have gone worse for the Kings or better for me. We won 3–1 and I scored the Rangers' final goal. It was my third goal in three games for the Rangers. The Forum crowd erupted in a loud, lengthy ovation, especially after I gave them a pumped fist.

It wasn't easy to be Rogie that night.

I had been nervous in warmups, and I didn't relax until I scored. "I love these guys to death," I told the *L.A. Times* after the game. "It was real tough tonight."

CHAPTER 6

LIVE FROM NEW YORK, IT'S SATURDAY NIGHT

WHEN LUC ROBITAILLE AND I used to take shifts of 90 seconds or longer in Los Angeles, we would joke to people that we weren't fast enough to get tired.

"We also have oxygen tanks on our back," I would say.

Once I joined the Rangers, I had no need for oxygen.

Roger Neilson was New York's coach and he didn't like it at all if I lingered on the ice too long. He wanted us to pay attention to detail, especially defensively.

My life on the ice with the Rangers was also different because the tight-checking Patrick Division style of play was a sharp contrast from the more wide open Smythe Division.

As an offensive player, I preferred the run-and-gun style that we played in Los Angeles. I went from a division where 8–6 and 6–5 games were normal to a division where 2–1 or 3–2 was standard fare.

Neilson always put one defensive-minded player on every line. Neilson didn't load lines like we did in Los Angeles. In L.A., we had scoring lines and checking lines. Neilson liked to balance his lines.

Just like Gretzky and Luc Robitaille, I knew my job with the Kings was to score, to contribute to the league's No. 1 scoring team. In Neilson's mix, the lines all had the same mission. That plan didn't always work as well as Neilson intended it to. We had a harder time creating offense and we weren't as strong defensively as Neilson wanted us to be.

One of my wingers that season was Troy Mallette. He had 305 penalty minutes that season. He was a hard worker, a good guy. But he was a fourth liner at best.

It wasn't as if I didn't know what to expect from Neilson. He coached the Kings for 28 games in 1984. I had seen his act before.

In March, the Rangers traded Ulf Dahlén and picks to the Minnesota North Stars for Mike Gartner. He ended up on my line and we clicked. Before he landed with the Rangers, he had already scored 40 or more goals six times. He ended up with 11 goals in 12 games to close out the regular season. When offensive guys play with other offensive guys you get better results.

The other major change for me was the Patrick Division was a lot more physical than the Smythe. It was a tougher division.

Even though it was a different world for me, I appreciated playing in New York for an Original Six team. Madison Square Garden was electric. Travel was much easier. We could bus to Philadelphia, Washington, Hartford, New Jersey, and Long Island. It felt like we had 60 home games. When I played there, I was told the Rangers spend 30 more nights at home than the Kings.

Off the ice, my adjustment to New York was smoother. The small-town boy lives in another major city. It had poker, horses, gambling, celebrities, and nightlife. It was perfect.

Not long after the trade, the Rangers were home in New York when Tom Hanks called me.

"What are you doing tonight?" Hanks asked.

Well, nothing, I was thinking. Our games at home were typically on a Friday night and then we were off Saturday because that's when the New York Knicks would play at Madison Square Garden.

He didn't wait for my reply.

"Do you want to come to *Saturday Night Live* with Rita and me?" Hanks asked.

"Can you give me a minute to think about it?" I said.

Within two seconds, I yelled. "Hell, yeah, I want to come."

I laughed. He laughed.

Hanks was hosting *SNL* that night.

"Bring your jersey," he said.

I had no clue what it was for. As the show was ending Tom came out to say goodnight with the cast and the musical guest, Aerosmith. He was wearing my jersey while waving to the audience and cameras. It shocked the hell out of me! Then he turned around and pointed to my name on the back of my No. 9 Rangers' jersey. I was sitting right there with his wife.

"Holy shit, this is cool!" I said.

Another time, I went out in Manhattan with actor Rob Lowe. I knew him from Los Angeles and invited him to watch a game at Madison Square Garden when he was in New York. I know our night on the town occurred after he had been engulfed by a scandal created by the leaking of a video of him having sex with teenager.

I know it was after his scandal because the next morning the *New York Post* published a photo of him and I clubbing. The caption read: "Let's go to the video!"

Back when I was playing in New York, players weren't allowed to live in Manhattan. I think management believed the city offered too many temptations. But I went into the city as often as I could.

Often, I found myself hanging out with teammate Ron Greschner and his supermodel wife Carol Alt. We golfed together. Ron was an okay golfer, and Carol was pretty good as well.

I remember we were playing a private course and Carol came out dressed in a skintight outfit. Everyone had their eyes on Carol.

Before we teed off, we went into the pro shop and the club pro said to Ron, "You know that we have a dress code here for women?"

"Yeah, I know," Ron told the pro.

"Well, don't say that if anybody asks you," the pro said. "You just didn't know."

I had numerous ways to get myself into jams. Nothing major, just the incidents that make for interesting reading in a book.

One of my friends had driven my Jaguar to New York for me. And the first time I was pulled over by the police, I didn't have my driver's license with me.

I told him who I was, and he asked me if I could prove I was Bernie Nicholls. I pulled my Rangers paycheck out of my wallet and showed it to him. He laughed.

He was a Rangers fan and didn't give me a ticket.

In Los Angeles, I didn't often receive any favors from the police. But in New York, and then when I was in Chicago, police would usually let me off with a warning for traffic issues.

When I played with the Rangers, all the players were given a card with the police chief's name on it that was supposed to help us on traffic stops.

Another time, a female police officer saw me parked. I had a female friend with me, and we were doing some stuff.

She tapped on the window. When I rolled it down, she said, "What are you doing?"

"Nothing," I said.

"It wasn't nothing," she said.

"Well, you know what we were doing," I said.

The officer saw the "police chief" card I had in my hand and asked to see it. She wasn't pleased. She threw it back at me. The card hit me in the chest. A scowl was on her face when she told me to get out of there now.

I gambled more often in New York than I did in Los Angeles, mostly because we had more players who liked to play cards in New York than we had on the Kings: Lindy Ruff, John Vanbiesbrouck, Ron Greschner, Chris Nilan, David Shaw.

Nilan, who we called "Knuckles," was a terrible card player, but the others were good players. We had plenty of fun playing cards. There was a Greek guy named Georgio who had a game in Greektown, and we would go down to his place and play for big money. Pots would get up to $2,500 or so.

Some people said Georgio was head of the Greek mafia. But I really don't have any idea whether he was or wasn't. I just knew he could make things happen.

One night, I remember we were playing and one of the players became enraged about something and rose out of his chair to leave. Georgio started gesturing and shouting something to him in Greek and the man returned to his seat.

"What the fuck did Georgio say to him?" I asked one of the players who spoke Greek.

"He said, 'If you walk out of here right now and continue to embarrass me in front of my friends, I'm going to shoot you in the back,'" the player told me like it was no big deal.

Holy fuck! Obviously, the guy took that threat seriously.

I had met Georgio by accident. I always gave away my sticks to kids. And in one of my first games in New York, I happened to give one of them to a young boy. I had no idea who he was. Two days later, I am coming out of a Rangers practice in Rye, New York, when two burley guys stop me in the parking lot.

"Mr. Nicholls, our boss wants to see you," one of them said.

They were polite. That's why I went with them. But I was kind of nervous.

Georgio was sitting in a limousine. He introduced himself and told me I had given my stick to his grandson. He was appreciative.

"If there is anything you need in New York, you come to me," he said.

Georgio asked if I like to play cards. When I said I did, he invited me to play in his game. When we hung out in Greektown everyone would cater to us. We had dinners with Georgio. I'm sure the poker games in his office were illegal. But it was awesome. During my two years in New York, I was set up for anything I wanted to do.

Any time I needed Mets or Yankees tickets, or a nice dinner, I just called Georgio

When I moved to New York, I ended up buying another house. It probably wasn't the wisest decision because I couldn't sell my $1 million home in Southern California. The combined monthly payment for the two homes was $15,000.

Adding to my aggravation was the fact that the purchase agreement on my house included a promise from the builder that four or five unfinished projects would be completed. But he never came back.

I called Georgio and told him I've got all these guys and they won't do what they're supposed to do. He said, "Okay, no problem." The next morning, 8:00, I get a knock on my door, and there's five guys out there ready to fix everything.

That was Georgio.

Tie Domi joined the New York Rangers as a rookie in 1990–91. When he was interviewed for this book, he told the story of a rookie exhibition game against the New York Islanders. Some of the veterans, including me, stayed to watch the game.

"I got into three fights and beat up three Islanders," Domi said.

Those details aren't in my memory. But I remember going up to Domi the next day and saying, "Good job, kid. Here's my car."

I told him he could use my car for the rest of training camp. Didn't tell him that it was a Jaguar. Imagine his shock when he walked into the parking lot and asked, "Which one is Bernie's car?"

Domi liked to have fun. This is how he tells the rest of the story:

"I always dreamed of being in the NHL, but it's another thing to be in New York City. Bernie was there: they called him 'Broadway Bernie'—he was the show. I think he realized I was there to protect him, and I don't think they had any protection before I got there for him. That was an old-school way of thinking.

"Guys like (Bernie) would take care of the guys who took care of them. When we went for dinners on the road, he would always take care of me, which I never really understood until I got older. And that was very kind of him. He was just that guy.

"Still, it was like, *Oh my God, this is really happening?*

"I hadn't even played a game yet, but being a Ranger, people were just so open. I'm going to parties and bars in this Jaguar convertible, and I didn't know anything about parking lots in the big city. I'd just park it on the road."

"I'll never forget driving down Seventh Avenue, looking up at Times Square, convertible down, hot chick in the passenger's seat…if there was ever to be a movie made about me that would be part of it!"

"I'd spent one night in the city, got up in the morning to drive back to Rye for practice, went outside and the car's gone. *Oh my God! What am I going to do?* I didn't see a sign the night before that said cars would be towed between 6:00 and 8:00 AM. And it's 8:30. I took a yellow taxi all the way to Rye.

"I never said anything to Bernie. He just gave it to me and never asked questions. Brian Leetch lived in the city so after practice I got a ride with him. I went to the impound and got Bernie's car out.

"When I got the car out, it was all keyed up on the passenger side. There was nothing I could do about it. It was New York City. I think it was like an initiation to the NHL. You take the good with the bad. It never even fazed Bernie. Anyone else would have snapped, but he just laughed it off."

I did appreciate that Tie looked after me on the ice, but that's not why I loaned him the Jaguar. I was just taking care of a young kid like the Kings veterans did with me. I remember Mike Murphy looked after me on the Kings. He would have me over for Thanksgiving and Christmas. We would play in Vancouver on December 23, and then we would have a home game scheduled for the day after Christmas. There was never enough time for me to go home, and I didn't want to disrupt my family's Christmas by inviting my parents to California. They had five children. The Nicholls family comes together on Boxing Day. I never wanted to take that away from them. That's why I appreciated what Murphy did for me. I wanted to pay it forward. I tried to do what I could for Tie.

I thought I played well in my first two seasons in New York. In 103 games over those seasons, I posted 110 points. We lost to the Washington Capitals in the playoffs in both seasons. In the first season, we lost in the second round.

In the second season, I put up 25 goals and 73 points. Defenseman Brian Leetch led the team in scoring with 88 points and I was next. I missed a few games because I broke my foot.

In the first playoff game, we won, and I scored the game-winner. I was playing with a broken foot that the medical staff froze to enable me to play. I scored twice and had four points in the third game, which we won 6–0 to take a 2–1 series lead. But they won the last three—two by one goal and 4–2 in the series clincher—without me playing at all because I tore my hamstring. The Capitals had a strong team.

And we did, too. I felt we had the better goalie. Mike Richter was unbelievable. We just ran into a better team.

Something funny happened at the end of the season. It was decided to rest some guys before the playoffs, and assistant coach Wayne Cashman was asked how we played. Cash said, "Look, if 18,000 fans can't get these guys to play I sure as hell can't."

That was the first indication that there might be changes.

Mark Messier trade talk was around all summer. He talked about possibly coming to New York. But I never thought about being traded. There was no talk or rumors about me that summer. Nothing.

Just to make sure, I had asked Rangers general manager Neil Smith if there was a possibility I would be dealt. I had finally sold my home in California at a loss. I didn't want to end up with two houses again. Smith told me he wasn't thinking about trading me.

My McNall promise hadn't spared me in Los Angeles. But I still believed Smith when he gave me the no trade promise. And when my wife became pregnant with twins and was going through a difficult pregnancy, I went back to Smith and asked again. He told me again that he wouldn't move me.

It seemed like Smith meant what he said. Summer ended and I remained a Ranger. We opened the 1991–92 season in Boston and we lost 5–3. I didn't have a point and I was minus-1. With 79 games to go, I wasn't concerned about one poor performance.

But the phone rang at 8:00 AM.

It was Neilson saying he wanted me to come and see him. Given the circumstances, I should have said, "Oh, shit." But I really didn't think I would be dealt. I wasn't the kind of player who gets traded twice in 21 months.

I believed that until Roger told me I been traded to Edmonton.

The deal was Mark Messier and Jeff Beukeboom (player to be named later) coming to New York for Steve Rice, Louie DeBrusk, David Shaw (player to be named later) and me. Messier and I were the principal players in the deal. At least I was still being traded for top players.

It was disappointing, nonetheless. And I was angry because doctors had put my wife on bed rest. I knew I couldn't leave her by herself.

One of my other thoughts was that I wished the Rangers could have acquired Messier without including me in the trade. I would have loved playing with Messier. I obviously knew him well from my days in the Smythe Division. We played him eight times per season.

Whenever someone asked me who the fiercest or toughest competitor in the NHL was, I'd always say Messier. I had unwavering respect for him.

Messier would do whatever it took to win a hockey game, whether it was score a big goal or ram someone through the boards.

But the biggest disappointment was leaving a team that I thought had turned the corner. With the arrival of Brian Leetch and goalie Mike Richter, I had started to believe the Rangers could contend. Turns out I was right about that, but I wasn't around to see it.

CHAPTER 7

FAMILY FIRST, OILERS SECOND

IN TODAY'S NHL, the media, coaches, and general managers are usually sympathetic, always understanding, when players have family medical issues.

Players often are given time off for the birth of a child, and it is not uncommon for players to be granted leave for medical issues.

That was not the case 30 years ago when I informed the Oilers I would not report to the team because my wife's doctor had ordered bed rest because she was expecting twins and her pregnancy had run into complications.

My New York home was approximately 2,450 miles from Edmonton. I wasn't going to leave my wife alone in New York to deal with the pregnancy by herself. She had an intravenous tube attached to her to keep a steady flow of medication.

Every Canadian player wants, or should want, to play for a Canadian team. But the timing was all wrong for me. My agent, Mike Barnett, agreed with me that I shouldn't report.

Barnett was Gretzky's former agent and was accustomed to fighting with Oilers general manager Glen Sather. But Slats, as he is called, was quite angry over not getting his expected return for dealing future Hall of Famer Messier.

My wife was seven months pregnant at the time of trade and my total fine was going to be $219,000 if she went full term.

This was before the Internet or social media, but I was not spared a public assault on my decision. One Edmonton columnist, noting my salary, wrote, "For $700,000, hire a nurse."

Apparently, some fans got the idea I didn't want to play in Canada, which wasn't true. But given my need to be home, Barnett did suggest that the Oilers may want to consider trading me to an American team if they didn't want to wait two months.

Some newspapers published a rumor about the Oilers considering trading me to Boston. Glen Sather and Boston's Harry Sinden were fishing buddies and they had previously done deals together. But who knows whether there was any truth to that.

Sather didn't let up. At one point, talking about me opting to stay with my wife, he told a newspaper reporter, "Squaws give birth in the prairies every day."

Imagine if he would say something like that in today's political climate.

But I stuck to my guns, and my twins—a daughter, McKenna, and son, Flynn—were born healthy on November 29. When I did arrive in Edmonton a couple days later, the fans just loved me because I'd done the right thing in their eyes.

It helped that Messier wanted out of Edmonton, and the fans believed I could replace Messier's offensive output. They had seen enough of me through the years playing in Los Angeles. Messier was 31 and I was 30 at the time of the trade. In 1990–91, Messier had 12 goals and 52 assists for 64 points in 53 games for the Oilers. In 1990–91, my totals were 25 goals and 48 assists for 73 points in 71 games for the Rangers.

But Messier was beloved in Edmonton. Make no mistake about it: had Messier not wanted out, Edmonton fans would have lost their minds over this trade.

The Edmonton media took note that I arrived wearing a fur coat and no socks. It was true, although there was an explanation. Once doctors gave me assurances that my wife and children were fine, I crammed stuff in a bag and caught a plane. I checked into the City Centre Suites and stayed there the rest of the season.

As it turned out, I loved absolutely everything about the city. I loved our team. I loved my linemates. I loved it all.

Truth be told, sitting in New York not doing anything had almost broken me. I was losing my mind. I couldn't wait to get to Edmonton. I was going home to Canada to play with an organization that I knew well because I played against it.

I think fans were sympathetic because Sather had fined me $200,000. Whether they had children or not, they understood why I stayed away. I put family ahead of hockey, and fans appreciated that.

When I arrived there, Sather was only a couple of years removed from coaching. He would still come down from his general manager's office and chirp at players if they weren't playing well. He had known plenty of success behind the bench. It didn't seem like he was ready to let it go. He'd go around the room and hit everybody.

Edmonton players had the most concern when I finally arrived in Edmonton. Players were told why I didn't come, but there were rumors that I didn't want to play for the Oilers.

The veterans called a meeting and captain Kevin Lowe addressed the situation head-on.

"We need to know: Do you want to be here or not?" he asked.

Everyone looked straight at me for my answer. I assured them that I definitely wanted to be there and explained the entire situation. I didn't blame them for wanting to know where I stood. Don't forget that this trade occurred in October 1991. That was only 17 months after the Oilers had won their fifth Stanley Cup in seven seasons.

The Oilers had moved out many of the key players from that team, including Wayne Gretzky, Jari Kurri, Paul Coffey, and Grant Fuhr.

I remember Barnett didn't like the idea of me playing in Edmonton because he felt they were a rebuilding team.

But the Edmonton players didn't see it that way, especially the veterans like Lowe and Craig MacTavish. They felt like they knew how to win and they could pass that along to their young talented players.

It hurt the Oilers that I wasn't there to replace Messier. I was glad we had a meeting to clear the air.

Sather had another concern: he was convinced that I was showing up severely out of shape. I had not worked out much in New York during those two months after the trade. I really had nowhere to go in New York. I was no longer a Rangers player, meaning I couldn't work out with New York players or use their facilities.

I did skate a little bit. Sather informed me I'd have to take a VO2 test, which measures your cardio fitness level by riding a stationary bike. Slats told me if I didn't pass, he was going to send me to the minors.

If I recall correctly, 60 is a really good score, and I recorded a 63. It was nothing for me because conditioning was probably always the best part of my game. I always had strong endurance. I felt as if I could extend shifts and never grow tired. So, I stepped right into the lineup, and it didn't take long to find my timing and get up to game speed.

And I was fortunate to play with a couple of dynamic forwards who could really skate and score: Joe Murphy and Vincent Damphousse. It stayed that way for the rest of the season, and we had an amazing run right through the playoffs. It was a special time for me.

I picked up an assist in my first game as an Oiler and we won at Vancouver. Two nights later we played San Jose, and I scored my first goal against the expansion Sharks at the Cow Palace in San Francisco, but we lost.

We lost there again a month later, but a couple funny events stand out from that day. I bought a purple velvet sports jacket in San Francisco while shopping with Petr Klima and we were late for the game because we missed the bus from the hotel to the Cow Palace.

And Sharks tough guy Link Gaetz fought Kelly Buchberger in a chippy game. Gaetz punched Kelly so hard it split one of those old Wilson helmets some players used to wear. They didn't offer much protection. Sather came into the dressing room after and was livid that none of us jumped in to help Buchberger. His rant ran even longer because we lost the game. Poor Kelly, he would fight anybody. My thought was: *Hey, players are coming to San Francisco, visiting a historic city and then have to play in that dump?*

We just wanted to get in and out of there. We were only 18–25–7 after that disappointing loss. It was starting to get late in the season, but we managed to pull it together. We won our next game, then lost, and followed that with six straight wins to pull within one of .500. After losing two in a row, we earned points in 13 of our final 18 games to finish third in the Smythe Division with 82 points. I scored 10 goals and 20 points in our final 18 games as my line with Murph and Damphousse finished strong.

And who do we meet in the playoffs? The Kings, of course! For the Kings it's "here we go again" playing the Oilers. It seemed like half the L.A. roster now were ex-Oilers so they're going to be excited. Paul Coffey, Jari Kurri, Marty McSorley, and Charlie Huddy. It's just ridiculous how many of Gretzky's former Edmonton teammates have joined him in L.A. We're going in, and I'm playing against the best in Gretz, and we're going into my home, L.A. We came in with a good group of guys, and we had offense to match theirs. They had home ice, and we went into the Forum and won Game 1. I had two assists in Game 1, two goals and an assist in Game 2, and two goals and two assists in Game 3.

I set an Edmonton team record with four power play goals in the series. That meant something to me because I was breaking an offensive record on the team Wayne Gretzky played for in his best offensive seasons. This is a guy who once put up 215 points in a season. Can you even imagine that level of production?

And then I ended up doing something he didn't. Not even No. 99 had tallied four power play goals in one playoff series.

Plus, I was thrilled to death because I did it against the Kings. Kelly Buchberger was all over Gretzky. The Great One struggled to find his points. He was held off the score sheet in three of the six games and had one point in Game 4. It was easier for us to start on the road than at home. Less distraction, more business. You watch the playoffs and good teams play great on the road.

I remember Craig MacTavish was making tee times halfway through the series in the next city we were going to play in. That's how confident we were. The Oilers were taught how to win there, and it grows on you. The next round, when we were in Vancouver, he'd made a tee time to play in Chicago because he figured out when we'd be there, and when we could play golf between Games 1 and 2. I led the team with five goals and 13 points that came in the first five games against the Kings. And we clinched the series in Game 6 when Billy Ranford shut them out 3–0 at home.

It was extra fun for me because Bruce McNall was in the stands along with all my fans in L.A. Maybe Bruce was thinking, *Maybe I shouldn't have traded that guy!* There's nothing better for an athlete to go back and beat the team that traded him away, especially in the playoffs when it ends your former team's season!

With 13 points in five games, I had plenty of say about the outcome. That was one of my favorite series for a lot of reasons. I helped my team win the series, and that's first and foremost. Then it's who we beat, and how well I played to beat them. When you're playing against the best in the world—whether it's Gretz or Mario Lemieux—and you dominate them at their game?

That's rewarding.

The second-round triumph against Vancouver was just business as usual for Edmonton. The Oilers were like a lot of great teams. They always had a mission. It didn't matter if we got beat 10–0, that's only one game. Just go win the next game. The Oilers' mission was to win that 16th game and do whatever it took to get there. Nothing fazed them.

We jumped out 3–1 in the series before the Canucks won Game 5 pretty handily on their ice. That was fine because we were going home. And, as a group, we knew we were going to win Game 6. And we did.

The series was similar to the one against the Kings. Vancouver had home ice like L.A. We went in and won Game 1 thanks to Joe Murphy in overtime, 4–3. You'll see a lot of times the better team will win Game 1. We knew as a group we were going to get it done, but until you do…it's 1–1 and we won Game 3. I had two assists and we got going again. You never know how it's going to go until you make it happen. We clinched it just like we did against L.A.: a 3–0 shutout from Ranford, who had another 26 saves in a clincher. You can't win in the playoffs without great goaltending, and we had that. From the word go we dominated Game 6.

We drew Chicago in the next round—the conference finals—and the Blackhawks dominated us.

My favorite place ever to play was Chicago Stadium. By the time I signed with Chicago later in my career the 'Hawks had moved into the United Center. So, I never got to play for them in the old building. It was my favorite place to play, and it wasn't even close. You'd climb up those narrow stairs from the locker rooms below the ice, step out onto the surface and there's 22,000 fans right on top of you. My line started Game 1 and we were matched all night against Chicago top defensive pairing—Chris Chelios and Steve Smith.

They had checking forwards Dirk Graham and Brent Sutter on us, too, and they beat the shit out of us all night. We didn't do much. I'll never forget standing for the anthems in that series. Chicago has a grand tradition in Chicago where the fans chant and applaud during the U.S. national anthem while the old organ is playing. You're standing there on the blue line and feeling so much pride. I had to put my head down because I was laughing. It was so loud and exciting that I put my head down because I didn't want people to see the laughter and get the wrong idea. It was the loudest I've ever heard it. That horn blared eight times that night. The Blackhawks beat us 8–2. They just hammered us.

We were never in that series. Chicago was too good; they shut us down and won in four straight. As much fun as we had in the other two series, we just ran into a buzzsaw against the Blackhawks. In the offseason the Oilers made a huge trade just before camp opened by sending Vincent Damphousse to Montreal for Shayne Corson, Brent Gilchrist, and Vladimír Vůjtek. And we really struggled out of the gate in 1992–93.

I missed Damphousse, who I considered one of the league's top younger scorers. I had 40 points in the first 46 games of the season, but I only had eight goals. I was still playing with Murphy, but we weren't the same without Damphousse.

What I loved most about my time in Edmonton was the total commitment to the team. They believed their winning tradition could carry them if they worked at preserving it. Sather liked to do outings as a team to continue their strong chemistry.

I remember he took everyone who wanted to go on a goose hunting trip. The team also went to Palm Springs to play golf with former President Gerald Ford. Every event had an element of team building.

Despite our rocky start, I ended up having a good relationship with Sather. He treated me very well. He said he would give me $100,000 of my fine money back for each round of the playoffs we won.

We won two rounds in 1991–92, which meant I got back the entire $200,000 I lost by staying with my pregnant wife. Sather was honest with me, telling me that the team was going to start to rebuild, and he planned to trade me to a team that would give me a chance to win a Stanley Cup.

I appreciated that. When you're older you never want to be in a rebuilding situation. The other news was that my wife Heather gave birth to another son, Jack, on November 25, 1992. We now had a newborn and one-year-old twins.

On January 13, 1993, Sather traded me to the New Jersey Devils for Zdeno Cíger and Kevin Todd.

At the time, I was Edmonton's leading scorer. I was going to turn 32 in a few months. Todd was 24 and Cíger was 23. Todd had registered 63 points the season before, but he only had 10 points in 30 games at the time of the trade.

Even though I enjoyed my time in Edmonton, this trade didn't disappoint me like the first two times I was dealt. The Devils had a good team. They could score and they had talent on the blue line. Scott Stevens was a beast on defense. Scott Niedermayer was a rising star. Herb Brooks of "Miracle on Ice" fame was the team's coach. This team looked like it was ready to make a move.

Trading me was just another in a long line of moves that told the Edmonton fan base that the Oilers' dynasty was coming to an end.

The 1992–93 season marked the first time the Oilers would miss the playoffs since merging from the World Hockey Association to the NHL in 1979. If not for the San Jose Sharks winning only 11 of 84 games in 1992–93, the Oilers would have been last in the Smythe Division.

But the Oilers had been a true dynasty. They had qualified for the playoffs for 13 consecutive seasons and won five Stanley Cups.

Compare that run to the Toronto Maple Leafs who haven't won a Stanley Cup since 1967, or the Calgary Flames who haven't won since 1989, or even the Vancouver Canucks or Winnipeg Jets who have never won a Stanley Cup.

Before missing the playoffs, the Oilers had played in 10 playoff rounds over three seasons. That included the 1990 Stanley Cup run. Remember that one was accomplished without Wayne Gretzky.

The Oilers were amazing for a very long time.

After my family arrived in Edmonton, I found a house on the west side of Edmonton.

I know what you are thinking: *YOU BOUGHT ANOTHER HOUSE AFTER WHAT HAPPENED IN LOS ANGELES AND NEW YORK?!*

No fucking way. I was a proud renter in Edmonton.

CHAPTER 8

UNIMAGINABLE SORROW

YOU DON'T GET OVER LOSING YOUR CHILD. At some point, you move on because there's nothing else you can do. But you don't forget the pain and sorrow.

Once the trade to the Devils was announced, my wife and I decided that it would be best for her to take our three children to Southern California where she would have her family to help her with our one-year-old twins and our newborn son.

Jack had been born with Down syndrome, a genetic disorder caused when abnormal cell division results in extra genetic material from chromosome 21. He was born prematurely and only weighed 3 ½ pounds at birth.

You want your family to be perfect, so initially you are devastated to find out that your child has Down syndrome. But I was playing in Edmonton where Joey Moss, who had Down syndrome, was the Oilers' dressing room attendant.

I thought the world of Joey and I realized that we were going to love Jack as well.

But after I had played two games for the Devils, I received a call that Jack had been taken to the hospital because something wasn't right. Doctors believed he had spinal meningitis. A doctor removed spinal fluid to check the diagnosis. Unfortunately, he removed too much fluid.

Poor Jack had a stroke. Jack was still alive, still functioning, but couldn't respond or react. He was deaf and blind. He was basically brain dead. We prepared ourselves for the worst.

Jack almost died that day, but doctors pulled him through. Two days later, that first Saturday, Jack improved. We were told he could be in that state for a while. I decided to fly back to New Jersey. But the entire time I was in the air, he had suffered seizures.

I went to Devils practice that morning, but my wife called again to say Jack wasn't doing well. Less than 12 hours after I landed in New Jersey, I was back on the plane to California.

Again, doctors pulled him through. They told us there was no hope, but each day someone at the hospital would tell us that he made some small bit of progress. It was hard to hear that, especially for my wife.

Our struggle to have children had been agonizing. Like too many couples, it just didn't happen for us. We even tried to adopt, and twice lost babies in that process because the mother changed her mind. Then we consulted a fertility expert and Heather gave birth to twins. Then, my wife became pregnant again four months after their birth.

We had no warning that Jack was a Down syndrome baby until after he was born. We had accepted that only to watch our baby become critically ill while we watched in horror. We took turns staying at the hospital and the sadness was overwhelming. He needed a feeding tube to get nourishment. It was tortuous to see him suffer.

I didn't know what to do. I decided to go back and play in New Jersey. Don't know if that was the right decision. Are there any right decisions at a time like this? My thinking was I couldn't help Jack. I tried to console my wife, but she was understandably inconsolable in this situation.

Right or wrong, after staying in California for two weeks, I returned to the New Jersey Devils in early February to play the next 11 games. I needed to let it go for a while. It was impossible to fully let it go. But you have to try. I tried to convince my wife she needed to get her mind off Jack, even for a short while. But she couldn't.

Somehow, with less than my usual focus, I scored goals in my first two games, and three in four. I managed to score five goals and 12 points in those 11 games.

Devils general manager Lou Lamoriello was kind to me, flying me back and forth to Los Angeles. Jack remained in the Long Beach Hospital because he needed so much care. We knew he was never coming home.

On November 20, five days short of his first birthday, Jack died.

It's impossible to describe the range of emotion I felt at that time. Sadness. Relief. Anger. Confusion. Guilt.

Jack had no life. He was there, but he wasn't. But you felt guilty for being relieved at his passing.

I didn't go to therapy when Jack died. I've never talked to anyone about his passing. That's not who I am. I don't talk about my feelings. I am like my father, George, in that regard. My father could be profound without saying anything. I could tell what he was thinking. I knew when he was disappointed, thrilled, or proud. He didn't need tell me what he was feeling.

I hope people will respect that I don't need to talk about how I felt about Jack and his death. As I like to say, I don't let anyone in my kitchen.

You can certainly tell how much his illness and passing impacted me by looking at my statistics that season. I played poorly. Maybe it was the worst stretch of my career. I scored five goals in 23 games, and I didn't manage to produce a single point in five playoff games against the Pittsburgh Penguins. I only managed three shots on goal. It's just impossible to keep your mind on your work at a time like that. You think you can compartmentalize your grief, but you truly can't.

What I do appreciate is how kind Lamoriello, coach Herb Brooks, and my teammates were in that period. It is not an easy situation for a team to deal with because they have a season to play. But they did all they could to help me get through it.

CHAPTER 9

DEVIL OF A TIME

WHEN I WAS DRIVING TO THE EDMONTON AIRPORT to fly to New Jersey, a local police officer gave me not one, but two, traffic tickets.

That's when it became painfully clear that I was no longer an Oiler.

The cop pulled me over because I was speeding to catch my flight. Still, it was surprising to me when the officer handed me a ticket. My first thought was the cop knew I was no longer an Oiler. He knew I had been traded. Otherwise, he probably would have given me a warning. I can't be sure of that. But I never received any tickets in New York.

Whether the trade colored his thinking or not, I was pissed after he handed me the citation. My reaction was to roll up my window and speed away. I spun out big time. And the bastard pulled me over a second time and gave me another ticket.

In hindsight, one of the best aspects of joining the Devils was getting to play for two revered coaches, Herb Brooks and Jacques Lemaire.

Even though I only had Herb for a short time, I loved every minute. He drew instant respect because he was coach of the U.S. squad that won the 1980 Olympic gold medal in Lake Placid.

But I can also verify that he can give the best pre-game motivational speeches I ever heard. He could talk about a horse, war, or historical event and have you on the edge of your seat the whole time.

He really could inspire you. Because of what was going on with my son, I wasn't playing well. I just couldn't get going. Herb called me into his office, and when I left, I thought I was Wayne Gretzky. He knows what to say. Herb was good at handling players and knowing how to use them in his lineup.

We were playing Pittsburgh in the playoffs and we were going over video. It's Lemieux this, Lemieux that. And Devils winger John MacLean started to laugh.

"John, what's going on here?" Herb asked.

"Well, Herb, you know, we have a Lemieux, too," John said.

It wasn't the 160 points Mario scored, but Claude Lemieux did lead us with 81 points.

"He ain't no fucking Mario Lemieux," Herb said. "I'll tell you that right now!"

Brooks just hammered him. He brought that out so quickly. That was Herbie.

Wish I could have given Herbie more. But flying back-and-forth to California took a lot out of me and my mind wasn't right because of what was going on with my son.

Not everyone loved Herb. At one point, he called Lemieux a "cancer" on the team. Herb wasn't fond of Russians. We had two legendary Russian players—Slava Fetisov and Alexei Kasatonov—on our defense. Herb didn't like them. It didn't help that I was in and out of the lineup and the team was struggling.

When Brooks didn't receive the assurances he wanted from management about his future, he resigned on May 30. I hated to see that decision, but I didn't know how much I would respect Lemaire.

My time with the Devils was memorable. When I was dealing with my son's illness, I played a game on Valentine's Day against the Philadelphia Flyers.

Paul Stewart was the referee. We were getting ready for the opening faceoff, and I was against Eric Lindros.

"Bernie, how are you doing?" Stewart asked.

"Great," I answered. "How are you doing?"

He acknowledged he was doing fine, and then said, "Big E, how are you doing?"

"Fuck off," Lindros said, "and drop the puck."

Stewart dropped the puck and Lindros cross-checked me. He just hammered me. Stewy gave him the two minutes he deserved. Not a minute later, Stewy wheeled Pelle Eklund into the box to give us a five-on-three power play.

In 2015, Lindros actually sued Stewart about something he wrote for a website that included mention of the faceoff incident. Stewart used the faceoff story to illustrate how his relationship deteriorated with Lindros.

Lindros said the article wasn't accurate, but I can testify that the faceoff story did happen.

In my second season in New Jersey I came in ready to play. I wanted to play better than I did in the first season. I was in excellent shape.

Jacques was one of the smartest coaches I had. He was a former Montreal Canadiens centerman. I think he designed his system based on how he used to like to play center. Under his system, the centerman went everywhere the puck went. He wanted the center to follow the puck like a magnet. If the puck went from one defenseman to another, the center went after it. As a center in Jacques' system, you better never turn your back on the puck.

He wouldn't let the defensemen pinch. His system was so regimented. He came from the Canadiens where he was part of eight Stanley Cups. Very smart, very well respected. Boy, did he put together a great team. Marty Brodeur made the team that season. It was defenseman Scotty Niedermayer's second season. What a team!

That season was a lot of fun for the players! It started with a little entertainment for me in training camp. John Campbell, the famed harness driver, and trainer Freddy Grant gave me a tip on horse running at the Meadowlands that night. Freddy was a huge NHL fan.

When I was playing for the Devils, I was living by myself and didn't go out much. But I did go often to the Meadowlands track on off nights.

The Devils had an exhibition game scheduled, but as a veteran player, I didn't think I would play. Imagine my surprise when my name was in the lineup.

I could have just gone over and placed a bet, but I wanted to see the race. So, I asked a referee to throw me out of the game. He went along with it. It was just an exhibition game.

That night, I did something to draw a minor penalty. I followed the referee like I was berating him, but I really wasn't. But he did his part by turning around and throwing me out of the game.

Perfect. Neither Lemaire, nor Lamoriello, ever found out. The tip did pay off and I won $3,600. I won the exacta as well.

I loved Lamoriello, even though he was too strait-laced for my taste. He was a stickler for the rules. He ran his team like we were in the army, everything by the book. That included a strict dress code. Players were required to wear a coat and tie on the road at all times. And I mean at all times.

We flew in late one night and arrived at our hotel. I had taken off my tie before I entered the lobby because it was stained. I was eating something, maybe on the plane, and I ended up with a food stain. You know how I feel about clothes. I'm not going to walk into a public place with a stained tie.

But Lou made no exceptions. He stopped me as soon as I got into the lobby.

"Where's your tie?" he asked.

"Lou, it's 2:00 AM, are you kidding me?" I said. "My tie had a stain on it."

He accepted my explanation, but he was pissed nonetheless.

In that season, the Devils went into every game believing we were going to win that game.

I'd say to Marty Brodeur, "You shut them out tonight, and I promise we'll get you a win."

I never played with such a talented player. Even as a rookie, he could deliver when it was needed most.

I broke both feet in my career blocking shots, and one time was that season. I played 61 games in the regular season. Not bad numbers—19 goals, 27 assists, and plus–24—to finish sixth on the team in scoring while missing 23 games.

And I had good linemates. A lot of the year I played with John MacLean and Claude Lemieux. We had great offensive players who might have had bigger numbers, but we obviously played great defense under Jacques' system. If we had that team in the old Smythe Division, I know those numbers would be a lot higher.

I'll never forget the 1994 playoffs. We opened against Buffalo and I got hit, not into the bench, but over the half boards. I tore cartilage in my ribs, and we lost Game 1 at home. I finished the game then spent the entire night in the hospital. I'm not sure how I got hit, but I tried to brace by holding onto the glass, but it was just out of reach. I had my arm up, I was reaching, and the boards got me right in the ribs.

That might have been the worst injury I ever had. I was in a lot of pain. They gave me Tylenol with codeine in it. I was so sore. You can't freeze something like that, so I wore a flak jacket when I played.

The Sabres had Dominik Hašek in net. It was a classic confrontation. If you think about it, that Hašek vs. Brodeur duel was probably one of the greatest goalie matchups in playoff history. Without question, both of those goalies have to be ranked among the top five all-time.

Marty and Hašek went toe-to-toe every game. The two of them only surrendered a combined eight goals in the first three games. We bounced back to win the next two games, both on 2–1 scores. But the pain was too much. I just couldn't play. I missed the next three games, including an epic four-OT loss at Buffalo in Game 6 that left the series tied 3–3. We outshot them 70–50 and lost 1–0. Hašek played brilliantly.

I made it back for Game 7, and that game was unbelievable, too. I had the primary assist on Claude Lemieux's goal midway through the second period that broke a 1–1 tie and stood up for a 2–1 final. We outshot them 46–18. We absolutely dominated the game, but we very easily could have lost it, too.

We drew Boston next. We felt confident because we had home ice. But the Bruins won the first two games. They were up 2–0 and now they were going home. Bruins defenseman Don Sweeney made a comment that appeared in the paper, "We want to get rid of these guys in a hurry, we've got some sore guys here who need rest."

Wrong thing to say.

We won the next four.

Those were close games, too, but we dominated Boston starting in Game 3. We won three of the last four by two goals and Game 4 was 5–4. Great teams play strong on the road, and we won three in old Boston Garden. I posted two assists in the clincher, including on the game-winner. We won 5–3 and outshot them 41–23. We were the better team.

Next up—Devils and Rangers—may have been the greatest series I ever played in. I say that even though we lost the series.

So much made this series interesting. The Rangers hadn't won a Cup in 54 years. The Devils had never won a Stanley Cup. It was only 11 miles from our arena to Manhattan. When we played in New Jersey, there were as many Rangers fans as Devils fans in our arena.

The Rangers had Messier, and that season they'd brought Mike Keenan in as coach. The Rangers loaded up with key players at the trade deadline: Glenn Anderson, Craig MacTavish, Stephane Matteau, Brian Noonan. They added talent and character.

But really, all the pressure was on the Rangers.

We stayed at the same hotel in Secaucus throughout the entire play-offs—all three rounds. We were just on the Jersey side, and not far from the Lincoln Tunnel that took you right into midtown Manhattan.

We left our cars at the Brendan Byrne Arena and checked into that hotel the day before the playoffs started. So, we were locked up and had nowhere to go. Lamoriello's rule: Players could spend the night after a game at their homes. But the next morning, players had to return to the hotel, practice, and check back into the hotel.

It was that way for two months. There was no going out, there was no nothing. That's the way Montreal did it, and Jacques brought that strategy to us. We'd bus to the rink and back. No distractions. All hockey. Focus only on the task at hand. I enjoyed it.

Stéphane Richer, a 36-goal scorer that season, scored late in a second overtime period and we won the first one at Madison Square Garden. I notched two assists in the third period when we scored twice to tie it. Our line got the tying goal in the final minute: Claude Lemieux scored at 19:17 with Brodeur pulled. Clutch.

We got outshot 41–16 in Game 2, and Mike Richter shut us out. The series was tied at a win apiece heading to our place. Not only did the Rangers grab Game 3, but I was suspended for cross-checking Alex Kovalev. I didn't receive a penalty when it happened, but they had it on film.

I hit Kovalev, and he stayed on the ice. I looked for the referee, but he wasn't watching. I'd cross-checked him right in the back of the head. What's funny is we were in the wives' room after the game and the TV was on. We were all depressed anyway because we lost, and we heard Mike Keenan doing an interview.

"This is bullshit," Keenan said. "This guy should be suspended!"

Keenan was always working the referees, lobbying for suspensions, and trying to make sure his team received the next call. Nobody worked the referees more than he did.

As I watched his theatrics on television, I'm thinking, *Holy shit. I didn't even remember doing it.*

It was the heat of the moment, and you could see me cross-check him. Sure enough, I got suspended for Game 4. We won that game to tie the series again. And we went into New York; I scored two goals and we took Game 5. I scored short-handed early in the first period and again on the power play midway through the third to give us a three-goal lead.

Up 3–2 in games, we had no business losing Game 6. We were up 2–0 late in the second period, Billy Guerin had the puck—and I'll never forget—he was going to dump it in and change. Everyone else was changing, and he was dangling with the puck. Sure enough, he turned it over at center ice. They went down 3-on-1, and Kovalev scored.

If we go into the third period up 2–0 with Marty—and the way our defense was playing—that game, and the series, is over. But we gave them a little life. Early in the third, Messier came down the wing. He took just a weak backhand shot on his off-wing and beat Marty. We were just shocked. For Marty it was absolutely just a bad goal. And that happens. He'd played unbelievable that series and that season. My God!

Then Mess scored again later in the third, and he got the empty netter. A third-period natural hat trick. We went from leading and the brink of reaching the Stanley Cup Final to a series-tying loss in the span of 20 minutes.

Everyone makes a big deal about how Messier "guaranteed" a win in the papers that day. We knew what he was saying. It wasn't bulletin board material. Mark knew they had a good team, and he just felt confident they would win. That's kind of what he said in the article. He was the ultimate captain.

I respect him for saying what he did because he was the first to do that. He was the ultimate captain. Now everyone guarantees a win and it doesn't mean anything. I think P.K. Subban did it a couple of times, but that doesn't matter because he wasn't the first.

The leader he was, Mark was telling his team, "We're winning this game." And they did. Again, Mark is the ultimate captain.

We absolutely should have won Game 6. We were the better team that night. We made a mistake and it cost us. Once they got it going, it wasn't good.

Brian Leetch scored midway through the second period of Game 7 to break a scoreless tie. And the Rangers were holding on for dear life late in the third. Somehow Valeri Zelepukin scored with eight seconds to go, and we tied it 1–1 just before the end of regulation. It reminded me of Claude Lemieux scoring late in the third period of Game 1 to tie that game, too.

We were really confident going into overtime. And the pressure was on them for sure. Later, as the game kept going, it kind of evened out before the end. I don't know who had chances in the first OT, but I know we all did. And it all came down to what was as bad a goal as you'd ever want to see.

Stéph Matteau scored from behind the net at 4:24 of the second overtime. He just sort of came out from behind the net, didn't really get in front, and backhanded it through Marty somehow.

Their mucking line was out there. Keenan played it right. He was giving his big guys a rest. I can still see it today. You just want to end a series like that with a nice goal.

But what a great series. Madison Square Garden went crazy. What an atmosphere that was.

The Devils-Rangers was never better than it was at that time. Brendan Byrne Arena in the Meadowlands was spacious, holding about 19,000 for hockey. We never drew very many fans just because the building was so big. But when the Rangers came the place would be packed.

I still do a lot of stuff for the Rangers. They bring alumni guys in. We sign autographs and Matteau's there all the time, too. He scored one goal that meant anything and he's a god. I love Stéph. That one goal was everything for him. Those kind of stories are always great.

My five-year contract I had signed back with the Kings was up, and the Devils were only willing to give me the $750,000 I was earning on my last season. The Blackhawks were more enthusiastic about how I could help them.

I thought the Devils were on their way up, and I believed they had a real chance to win the Stanley Cup. They could have easily won it in 1994. But Chicago was another Original Six team and the $1 million the Blackhawks were offering seemed liked real money.

I would have loved to stay in New Jersey but playing in Chicago was as good as it gets.

CHAPTER 10

THANKS A MILLION

MY HEAD WAS IN THE CLOUDS both literally and figuratively when I signed a two-year free agent contract with the Chicago Blackhawks paying an average of $1.15 million per season.

Making $1 million isn't such a big deal in today's NHL, but it was very meaningful back then for a small-town Canadian boy who was always thankful to be paid to play a game he loved. I must be doing all right if a team was willing to pay $1 million to have me as one of their centers. I celebrated my new deal by buying an apartment on the 89th floor of the John Hancock building in downtown Chicago. I swear there were days I'd wake up, look out my window, and the clouds were below me.

The view was magnificent. Talk about having your own slice of heaven.

Blackhawks teammate Joe Murphy lived around the 60th floor and comedic actor Chris Farley lived about five floors below me.

It would have been a perfect setup for the 1994–95 season if not for the fact that the owners locked us out because negotiations for a new collective bargaining agreement had gotten bogged down. The players' hope was that the season would start late, but we would end up playing close to a full season. But the lockout dragged on and on.

When an agreement was finally reached, we started the season on January 20, 1995, and only played a 48-game regular season.

That meant my first salary of more than $1 million turned out to be a pro-rated salary of $628,571, which was actually less than I was paid on my previous contract. I just couldn't catch a break in that regard. I had to wait until 1995–96 to earn more than $1 million for the first time.

The 1994–95 season was memorable for a variety of reasons, including the fact my friendship with Chris Chelios helped me get into the best shape of my career. Plus, I got to play for coach Darryl Sutter, one of six Sutter brothers to play in the NHL.

That was Darryl Sutter's first year as head coach. We started 19–9–2 before running into a wall with a 13-game winless stretch (0–10–3). We turned it around just in time, winning our last five games to finish third in our division and qualify for the playoffs.

For those who know Sutter, you can imagine what an emotional rollercoaster you are riding with Darryl as your coach on that kind of up-and-down season.

I love Darryl. Always have. But he is hyper. Darryl is the first coach I ever had who wanted his players to stretch *before* practice. On game day, we were expected to be stretching at 9:45 AM sharp in preparation for a 10:30 morning skate.

That was just a little early for Murphy and me. We always drove in together, and our routine was to stop and buy a milkshake at a restaurant right by the United Center.

One day, we arrived right at 9:45. Rather than be late, I dropped to the floor in my street clothes, milkshake in hand, and started to stretch.

When Darryl came into the room, he wasn't happy.

"Look at you fucking guys!" Sutter said. "You're not ready for fucking game night? You're not ready, right?"

This was early in the season. I'm thinking, *I'm not ready yet, I don't play for like 10 hours. I'm not even close to being ready!*

But that was Darryl. Always intense. Nothing wrong with that. I always said he had an urgency when it came to details. He was prepared enough for everybody.

For example, we'd always have game sheets, pages, and lists of statistics about the Blackhawks and our opponents. There was always a kid from the other team who had just been called up. He'd call on one of his players and ask, "This John Doe guy is up, what do you know about him?"

When no one could tell him anything about the new player, Darryl would proceed to inform us what the kid ate for breakfast, what his mum and dad did for a living, where he went to school, the name of his first girlfriend. He knew everything!

If Darryl was coaching your team, you were always well prepared. Playing against Chicago under Darryl was always really tough. I felt like he had his guys really wound up. And Darryl was always whistle-to-whistle. If you took a dumb penalty, or something after the whistle, Darryl would lose his mind on you.

Everybody's different—some guys can take it and some can't. If Darryl yelled at defenseman Gary Suter? He was done. We were playing in Hartford and Darryl ripped Gary's stick out of his hands and he then wrote "W-O-R-K" right on his stick. Gary played the rest of the game with that stick.

Darryl and our eccentric goalie Eddie Belfour butted heads constantly. We had to be on the ice at 11:00 AM for practice. Eddie would be following his odd routine and come out a couple minutes late. Darryl would be waiting at the door for him. As soon as Eddie set foot on the ice, Darryl would say, "Okay, line up and shoot, Eddie, get in the net."

Normally we'd stretch out and skate first. Instead, we'd just start shooting pucks. Eddie would leave the net because he hadn't stretched or warmed up. Then they would clash.

They would have "fuck you" fights on the bench. Darryl loved it. He loved confrontation. Darryl really did love his players. He honestly *really* did. If our team was doing good Darryl was hard on us. He'd do whatever was necessary to keep us there, and sometimes he believed it meant being hard on us. But if we were having a hard time for whatever reason, he recognized when it was time to back off. He was good in that regard.

Darryl may not have liked how I lived away from the rink, but he liked me. He appreciated how hard I played. Darryl is a family man. He did what he could to help players take care of their family. I had the twins, and they were still young. When the Blackhawks headed for a Western road trip, he would let me go a day early.

One of the rewards of playing in Chicago is that I had the chance to play with defenseman Chris Chelios. Obviously, I always wished I could spend more time playing with Wayne Gretzky. That would have been amazing. But I've said if I had to pick one guy to be my teammate it would have been Chelios. No one worked harder on and off the ice. I hate to lose, but Chelios can take that attribute to its highest level.

One time, Chelios cut my ear for nine stitches because I tried to go around him in practice. Chris would play you as hard in practice as if he did in a playoff game. He only weighed 185 pounds, but pound for pound no one was tougher or meaner.

I got to know Stevie Yzerman at the World Championships and I really liked him. But I could do nothing to spare Yzerman pain when he played Chicago. When the Blackhawks played the Red Wings, Cheli would whack the shit out of Yzerman in front of the net. He would hammer him, punch him, cross-check him, annoy him to death. One night, Yzerman lost it and tried fighting Chelios. Yzerman was so pissed. That was Cheli at his best. He would do that to any player that he deemed a threat to beating us.

A Chicago native, Cheli owned Chicago. I don't remember how many concerts we went to together. But when we went to a concert in Chicago, the red carpet was rolled out for Cheli. Cheli was a god at the United Center. We attended a Rolling Stones concert one night and got escorted right to the front of the stage. Everybody in Chicago loved Cheli.

The other benefit of playing with Chelios was that he changed my conditioning habits. It was a different era and players didn't work out the way they do today. But Chelios did, even back then.

He got me and Joe Murphy working out with him and Gary Suter, another fitness devotee.

We'd work out in the sauna, all of us in there together, doing pushups and sit-ups. We'd keep track of how many we could do. Cheli would initiate it. We'd do a set of pushups, 10, 20, 30, 40, 50, 60, and 70, and then work our way down. We'd time our sit-ups. I was at 80 or 90 per minute.

Even on the road, we'd arrive in the hotel and head straight to the sauna. I loved it. Before then, my conditioning was natural. I played baseball in the offseason, and that would help, and then I would skate starting in August. But Chelios got me more interested in working at my conditioning. I've said before I wish I would have started earlier.

At 33 years old, I led the Blackhawks in scoring with 22 goals and 51 points in the 48-game schedule. I scored 10 points more than anyone. I had three memorable road games in 1994–95: four goals and two assists in Vancouver, four goals in L.A., and three goals at San Jose.

The cool aspect about scoring four goals in L.A. was being in the dressing room after the game, knowing that many of my Los Angeles friends had been there to watch.

The usher would come in and say people were waiting to see me.

"Kurt Russell wants to see you," an usher said.

I yelled out the door, "I'm not coming out unless Goldie is there."

Then I heard a woman's voice saying, "I'm here, I'm here!"

Chris Farley had come from Chicago to Los Angeles. He came into the Blackhawks dressing room, wearing my jersey with ketchup and mustard splattered on it. He had his hair slicked back. He was wired on who knows what. It was just another typical night mixing with the Hollywood celebrity scene.

Another fact I learned in Chicago is that Belfour was among the league leaders in intensity. Like most goalies, he had quirks. He wouldn't let anyone touch his skates. He worked on every aspect of them, including the sharpening. During the playoffs he wouldn't leave the rink until 1:00 AM because he had to have all his stuff perfect. Goalies are different. He had to get everything set up right.

One night we'd gotten beat, and Belfour was an angry man. There was a brand-new, high-tech, $5,000 projector in the room with a big screen that hung from the ceiling. He took his goalie stick and shattered that projector. Did he get in trouble for that? Oh, I think he did! He was crazy.

The Blackhawks played Toronto in the first round when the Leafs were in the West. It was a great series. I didn't score a goal but had assists in five of the seven games. Murph had a great playoff run. He scored nine goals in the playoffs and did damage late in that series.

We lost the first two games at home but bounced back to win the next three: both games in Toronto, and Game 5 back at home. We lost Game 6 but were back in the United Center for Game 7, where we were confident. Murph scored two big goals, Denis Savard had a three-point game, and we won 5–2.

I remember our power play was sharp all season. At one point, we were 24 percent. We had Jeremy Roenick, Tony Amonte, Murph, and me, along with Suter and Chelios crammed in Darryl's office for a meeting.

"Okay, look, I didn't play on the power play," Sutter said. "This is your power play. You work at it. Make it work."

That's all he said. And it made so much sense. Darryl couldn't teach us how to make it work. He knew the game, but power play often relies on offensive instincts. A coach can draw up 50 plays. But what works best is when players read what's happening on the ice, sense who is going where, and then react accordingly. Darryl knew that he never possessed the offensive instincts that made you exceptional on a power play. But he also knew you can't teach them anyway. That's why Darryl is quality. He knew where he could make an impact and where he couldn't.

All Darryl wanted from his players was that they worked hard when they were on the ice. If they didn't, Darryl would put someone on the ice who would.

Our power play carried us in the regular season and into the playoffs, especially in the next series against Vancouver. We swept the Canucks, but all the games were close and three went into overtime. Murph struck on that dangerous power play to win Game 1 in overtime.

We shut them out in Game 2, and Cheli scored in overtime in each of the last two games to end the series. I set Cheli up in OT of Game 3. I was in the right corner behind the net and Cheli snuck in. I got him the puck, and it was like a mini break for him from just inside the hash marks. He read a play as well as anyone, but he didn't jump in like that very often.

I wasn't on the ice for it in Game 4, but for Cheli to score another overtime goal was a pretty cool moment. In Chicago, Cheli was my boy. I loved watching him score another overtime goal.

The nice thing about the second-round sweep was we had some rest before the next round. Turned out against Detroit, it didn't matter. The scores were close, but they shouldn't have been. It went five games. All four of Detroit's wins were by a single goal. Belfour was ridiculously sharp. Without him, it would have a lopsided sweep. Not even close.

In the offseason, Craig Hartsburg was hired to replace Sutter. That wasn't a good trade for me. For whatever reason, we didn't connect like Sutter and I did.

I roomed with tough guy Bob Probert that season. Considered one of the NHL's all-time greatest fighters, Probert signed with Chicago a week after me the previous year but ended up in drug and alcohol rehab and didn't play that season.

Bob was a big part of a team bonding early in the 1995–96 season. Everywhere I played we always had Super Bowl parties and Super Bowl pools. NHL players will put together a gambling pool on almost anything. In this season, we put together a pool to guess the verdict and sentence of O.J. Simpson.

I don't remember how much we put in—maybe $20 a person—to pick what Simpson's verdict and sentence would be. Our predictions were all written down on the white board in the dressing room. We all watched the proceedings on television. Hell, the whole world was watching it. I think all sports stopped to watch it.

Bob was the only player who said he'd get off. According to Bob, Simpson would be acquitted.

Almost everyone told Bob he was nuts. Not a chance in hell, we said.

"What are you thinking, Bob?" I asked him.

Of course, Simpson was acquitted, and Bob won the fucking pool. I thought it was an incredibly fun team-bonding moment. Everybody enjoyed Bob's I-told-you-so moment. Bob was a nice man. We lost him way too early. I miss him.

We played well in 1995–96, finishing second in the Central Division with a 40–28–14 record. This was a good team and I thought we had a shot to win at all. Word was that left wing Wendel Clark and puck-moving defenseman Mathieu Schneider were available at the trade deadline. I publicly lobbied for the Blackhawks to acquire them.

Hartsburg called me out in front of the team.

"You're saying Bob [Probert's] going to have to play on the fourth line or sit out?" he asked.

"If we get a better player who will help the team then so be it," I answered.

I felt like we were one or two players away from winning it all. If someone has to take a reduced role to make us a better team, then we should do it. Aren't we here to do whatever we can to win? The coach should be preaching that. I shouldn't have to tell him.

My answer shut him up a little bit. But he didn't like it much.

In this season, I also lacerated my spleen and missed 22 games from early November through late December. It happened on a play when I was the player making the hit. I caught Colorado's Valeri Kamensky with his head down and laid him out. The problem was our heads collided and my stick got stuck in my ribs. My head was spinning, it felt like my eyes were stuck. I was dizzy, my shoulder was sore, and I barely made it back to the bench.

I swept the cobwebs out and finished the game. As I was getting checked out afterward that's when we realized what it was. I was sent to the hospital right away, and I couldn't do anything until I healed. I couldn't even leave the hospital. I was there for a couple weeks.

I finished with 19 goals and 60 points in 59 games and was fifth on the team in scoring. Cheli led with 72 points. Cheli and I were both 34 years old. Considering I was a point-per-game player, I would have probably led the team had I not missed those 20 games. I felt like I had an exceptional season.

We finished second to Detroit, who just ran away with the President's Trophy race in the regular season. The Red Wings lost only 13 games and totaled 131 points. We were next with 94. It wasn't even close. But we swept Calgary in the first round. I had a goal and an assist in the first game. We won the next two easily before Murph scored halfway through the third OT of Game 4 to clinch it.

Colorado was next, and they were good. That's in the middle of their rivalry years with Detroit, and we had them. We were up 2–1 in the series with Game 4 at home, then Cheli pulled a groin or did something. The medical staff tried everything, even tried to freeze it. Cheli tried to skate but couldn't. He kept falling down. There was no quick fix or getting anything to work for what he had.

We lost Game 4, 3–2. We were right with them. If we'd won Game 4 at home, we'd have been up 3–1 in the series. It was a great game, but we didn't have our best player. That was a big blow for us. We lost Games 5 and 6, the last one in double overtime.

Then my time with the Blackhawks was finished. I didn't want it to be. I loved playing in Chicago. But salaries were starting to rise dramatically in the NHL and Blackhawks owner Bill Wirtz didn't want to pay those salaries.

I didn't really know Mr. Wirtz. I knew his son, Rocky Wirtz, well. He's hands-on, similar to how Bruce McNall was in L.A.

But back then Bill Wirtz was in charge. I know guys had some good run-ins with him, especially back in the day. He owned Chicago. Bob Pulford was the general manager, and he ran the tight ship that Mr. Wirtz wanted. I don't know if Hartsburg had a say with who was kept, but I know Murphy signed a $9 million deal with St. Louis. And Jeremy Roenick was traded to Arizona after a contentious contract negotiation.

But on July 1, the start of free agency, general manager Dean Lombardi made it clear the Sharks wanted me.

Dean had a solid plan. The Sharks were anticipating skilled and speedy Patrick Marleau stepping into the lineup, plus other young prospects. His idea was I'd mentor them. And when Patty was ready to take over, I'd take a lesser role. I loved that idea. I was going to be 37, 38 years old at the end of the contract, and if I needed to be your No. 1 center at that age we'd be in a whole lot of trouble. I was realistic about what I would be like at that age.

I did talk to the Mighty Ducks of Anaheim. I actually came close to signing there. My children had been living in Southern California. The family didn't move with me to Chicago. A move to the Ducks would have brought me back to the Hollywood scene.

But I loved the Sharks' plan too much. I signed a three-year contract with San Jose for what I considered big money: $1.2 million over the first two years and then an option for the third season.

For me to go to San Jose was a perfect fit. I loved Southern and Northern California. I wanted to play in the NHL until I was 40 and Dean had laid out a plan that would help me get there. I'd start out as a top six forward and then gradually become a role player and teach the kids.

Saying goodbye to Chicago was difficult. It was a smart decision I made going to Chicago, even though the Devils ended up winning the Stanley Cup the season after I left. That's a regret I have to live with. But how crazy is it that I grew up in such a small town and ended up playing in the major cities of Los Angeles, New York, and Chicago? Not only that, but I fit in every city as if I had lived there my entire life.

Chelios and I became close friends. He owned his own bar in Chicago called Cheli's. It was popular with fans. The place would be packed after games, and I often jumped behind the bar to help out. It was perfect for the guy who didn't drink. Of course, I had to learn to mix drinks. But it was loads of fun.

Honestly, there's not a better sports city in the world than Chicago. And there's no better city.

Terrific golf courses. And we could play any time we wanted. We went to Bulls, White Sox, and of course the Cubbies games.

One time, the White Sox invited us to come to a game and take batting practice. Robin Ventura pitched to us. And yes, I did clear the fence.

I had the southwest corner view from my 89th floor apartment. I could see the Miracle Mile, the rink, and a corner of Lake Michigan.

I knew Michael Jordan from the celebrity golf tour, but I got to know him better hanging out with him in Chicago. When our season was delayed by the lockout, we went down to Arizona to watch him play baseball in the fall instructional league. We hung out with him for four or five days.

He always treated me well. He was especially kind when I brought my old high football coach Gary Brohman to town. I took him to a Bulls–Atlanta Hawks game early enough to catch Jordan just shooting on the court at 4:00. I walked on the court with Gary and his two boys and introduced them as "my friends from Haliburton, Ontario."

Michael ended up posing for a photograph with them. That was 26 years ago. But that photograph still hangs on the wall in Gary's basement.

The game against the Atlanta Hawks was tight. There was a TV timeout with a minute left. And Michael happened to be right in front of the Brohman family. He looked down at Gary's son, Pete, who is 6-foot-4, and said, "Stand up, Peter."

He remembered his name.

"Do you play basketball or hockey back in Haliburton?" Michael asked.

"Mr. Jordan, I play hockey," Peter replied.

"I'm going to tell you something, Peter," Michael said. "I make a helluva lot more money than Nicholls. You should take up basketball."

CHAPTER 11

TAMING TIGER

I'M REASONABLY CONFIDENT I'm the only person to have scored 70 goals in an NHL season and beat Tiger Woods in a golf match.

That is a rare double.

The triumph over Woods occurred in the early 1990s when we had set up a match at the Big Canyon Country Club in Los Angeles between former California Angels and former Los Angeles Kings players. As I recall, it was Jimmy Fox, Mark Hardy, me, and a club member named John Hamilton.

We were up against Bobby Grich, Doug DeCinces, Fred Lynn, and two other players I can't remember.

Our group was short a golfer. With the starter trying to hurry us along, Hamilton asked if I saw who was on the driving range.

It was Tiger Woods.

"Why don't you ask him if he wants to play?" Hamilton said. "All he can say is no."

But he said he would play. So here comes Tiger with his golf bag, which he throws on my cart! At the time, he was maybe 17 or 18 years old. It was pretty fun to ride around with Tiger for 18 holes!

Tiger Woods had not joined the PGA tour yet, but we all knew who he was. One moment I will never forget is Hardy trying to give Tiger golf tips.

"You know, Tiger, if you tee the ball up higher you might hit it a little bit further," Hardy said.

Think about that in terms of what Tiger ended up accomplishing. He is arguably the greatest to ever play the game and a hockey player is giving him a tip?

Hilarious!

When the round was over, I'd shot 72, while Tiger carded a 74. I beat Tiger! The guys on the team all chimed in, "Bernie beat Tiger!"

That's my golfing claim to fame. I beat Tiger Woods.

In the retelling of this story, I conveniently leave out the part where he is just a teenager. A year or two after our round, Tiger shot an 11-under-par 59 to break the course record by five strokes.

Golf is another of my passions. I didn't start playing until I joined the Kings. I didn't start playing regularly until I was about 25. I actually recorded my first hole in one on my 25th birthday. It was the 9th hole at Industry Hills Golf Club in L.A. When I hit it, I knew it was headed toward the pin. But I didn't know it went in until I walked up to the hole.

When I first started to golf, it was with teammates Morris Lukowich and Grant Ledyard. We always gamble when we play, usually in a skins game format.

None of us were really any good, so everyone was competitive on every hole. We'd play $10 for the first six holes, $15 the next six, then $20 for the last six holes. It could get a little crazy, but it was always fun.

Once I started playing, I improved dramatically and quickly. At the time I played with Tiger I was a five-handicap. Today, I'm a one-handicap. My low round is 65 and I can consistently shoot in the high 60s if I'm playing regularly. I have five holes in one.

One of my holes in one came at Kapalua in Hawaii where the pros play their season-opening tournament. All the past season's winners get to play the first event of the year. My ace came on the 8th hole, 180 yards. I stuck a 5-iron in there and witnessed the ball go in the cup.

To ace a hole where pros play, and a big one like that, that felt great. The other four were shorter holes. So the one at Kapalua is probably my favorite because of where it happened.

It made sense to me that I should be able to golf well, because I have good hands for both hockey and baseball. Plus, I have good hand-eye coordination.

I improved to the point that I finished third at one tournament on the celebrity tour in the Cincinnati area. I also won a doubles tournament with Jun Lee, who is a teaching pro in San Jose. Because my partner didn't show up, tournament officials let me team with her.

Plenty of NHL players are quality golfers. Dan Quinn is one of the best I ever played against. He won the famed American Century Celebrity Golf Classic at Edgewood Tahoe Golf Course in Lake Tahoe five times. Some other former NHLers who can play are Pierre Larouche, Gary Leeman, Mario Lemieux, Grant Fuhr, and Jeremy Roenick. I've played with Gretzky a few times as well. He loves to play. I don't think I've met a hockey player who enjoys golfing as much as me. But Gretzky is close.

Larouche is an excellent player and colorful character who once said he was paid his $150,000 salary to score goals. "If they want me to play defense, they can pay me another $150,000."

He can hustle you on the golf course. One time, Leeman and I took on John Vanbiesbrouck and former major league manager Davey Johnson. We played the match because Larouche said Johnson was a five-handicap like the rest of us.

It turned out that Johnson was close to being a scratch golfer and he was the difference in our match at Sleepy Hollow Golf Course in Briarcliff Manor, New York.

I tried to gain some revenge by bringing in a ringer in a match against Larouche. It was pro golfer Aaron Meeks, who played on the Asian PGA Tour.

But Pierre thwarted my plan by shooting a 68. Meeks shot 73 and I shot 71. I lost a couple of hundred bucks in both of those matches, but you have to tip your hat to Pierre.

Tiger Woods is not the only non-NHL celebrity I've played with. I remember playing with Michael Jordan on a day when his Chicago Bulls had a home game. This was when the Bulls were winning championships. We played nine holes and then that night M.J. lit it up for his Bulls. He didn't even play in the fourth because the Bulls owned such a big lead.

That's what a great player can do. To watch him golf and then play so well that night was so cool!

Michael was fun to play with because he loved to gamble as much as I did. I could beat him in golf, but he'd get his money back playing gin. The man was as dominant in gin as he was on the hardwood.

I remember getting M.J. good on the golf course one day and he insisted on playing cards afterward. He got his money back in a hurry.

Another time, I was up on him on the front nine and he said he wanted to go double or nothing on the back nine.

"Are you sure you can afford it?" I joked.

"Yeah, I think I can," he said, laughing.

When you gambled with Michael Jordan, you had to remember that he had no breaking point. Everyone I knew had a breaking point—the point where you know you can't afford to be risking that money.

I don't care who you are, when you reach that point, you aren't going to do as well. The pressure is too much. But there isn't a price that's going to intimidate Michael. We never played for big money. We played for just enough money to make it interesting. It was more for fun.

Once I got hooked on golf, I became quite obsessed with it. When I joined a club in Los Angeles, I would play every day. I'd even play on game days. I knew I needed to be careful. I would ride in a cart. I remember playing 18 holes the day we played a Russian touring team who came for a series of exhibitions against NHL teams.

In San Jose I had a house on the course and brought my own cart. The Sharks had given me it as a gift when I played my 1,000th game. It had leather seats and a big shark fin on it. And the most important accessory was surround sound speakers.

I would drive with music blaring. People would call the clubhouse every day to complain I had the music on too loud. I think they were just jealous. When I found out people were complaining I just turned the music louder.

When guys retire, they've got to have something they're passionate about. I still work on my golf game to this day. I won't do anything I'm not good at. I work hard at it. I've got great friends who are golf pros. I think Hank Haney is as good a teacher as there has ever been. He worked with Tiger Woods. I'll bug him every now and then for help on my game.

I've got a couple guys in Vegas: Eric Meeks, who won the U.S. Amateur in 1988, and his brother, Aaron Meeks. They help me out. Golf is a complicated, funny game. You can shoot 65 one day, then 78 the next. Some days you are dialed in and other days it's like you've never played the game before.

Golf is addicting. I always go out with guys and bet, just to have something on the line. I've always said, "I don't want your money, I just want your pride." I don't care if we're playing for $1. It doesn't matter. I just want you to know I beat you.

Golf is a great way to meet people. I do so many charity events that involve golf. It's a good chance for someone to play with a fan or a sponsor. It's so good that way.

I played a skins game in San Jose with Freddie Couples, John Daly, Craig Stadler, and John Cook at San Juan Oaks. I caddied for Craig the first day. They played nine holes in the morning and had lunch after the round. Then, when everyone had left, that group hit the back nine just for practice and asked me to play with them. John Daly gave me his driver and lent me some clubs.

The next day I caddied for Freddie. I knew Freddie just a little bit. He was a big sports fan. I don't know if there's a better pure golf swing than his. I was so fortunate with the things I got to do.

One summer Craig Stadler was having a big golf tournament in San Diego. I was there with Kings owner Bruce McNall. There was an auction for a golf package in Lake Tahoe, which included a stay in Caesar's Palace, then a private jet flight to Pebble Beach to play Cypress Point—one of the most exclusive courses around. Everyone was bidding on it. And I bid—with Bruce's money—and won it for $20,000.

It was supposed to be for Stadler, Bruce, Gretz, and myself. But Gretz couldn't make it. We flew Bruce's helicopter right along the ocean shore from San Diego to L.A. and dropped Gretz off first. Then we flew right through the city and dropped me off at the Friendly Hill Estates house.

When it came time for the trip, John Candy joined us in place of Gretz. I spent four days flying in a private jet, playing golf, and staying at Caesar's Palace in Tahoe. We went to a boxing match. We had John with us and were seated right up front.

I golfed a few times with Peter Pocklington, who owned the Edmonton Oilers. He cheated! Everybody knew it. He always wanted to play for money. He'd hit a ball, and everyone could see it was out of bounds. He'd drive his cart up and down and, all of a sudden, he'd yell, "Got it, got it!"

When he marked his ball on the green, he'd grab his ball and throw his coin toward the hole four or five feet. Everyone was doing their thing, and you look up and notice, "Hey, you're up, Peter."

He'd walk way up closer to the hole when you knew his ball was really further away.

You had to watch him. He never lost a ball.

He'd hit the middle of the lake.

"Better re-tee, Peter," you would say.

Me in my rookie year. *(Jayne Kamin-Oncea/ USA TODAY Sports/ Imagn)*

March 9, 1982: I scored my first career goal against Glenn "Chico" Resch. He actually signed his goalie stick from that to me. And amazingly, this was sent to me by a fan who took the photograph from the stands.

Three Kings: (from left) Luc Robitaille, me, and Steve Duchesne pose on Venice Beach. *(Andrew D. Bernstein/Getty Images)*

Me and my dad hunting.

The first moose I ever bagged with a bow and arrow.

Me with my Utah elk antlers.

Me and dad.

At the Annual Sports Spectacular benefit dinner at the Century Plaza Hotel in Los Angeles on July 16, 1989. From left, there's: me, winner of the hockey award; Dick Butkus, life achievement award; Magic Johnson, basketball award; Dick Enberg, sports journalist of the year award; and Tim Brown, football award. *(Mark J. Terrill/AP Images)*

May 23, 1994: Celebrating my second goal of the game with teammates Stephane Richer and Scott Stevens at Madison Square Garden. *(Ron Frehm/ AP Images)*

Playing for the Blackhawks in a game against the Dallas Stars. *(Joe Patronite/Allsport/ Getty Images)*

With John Candy in the dressing room.

Tom Hanks wearing my jersey on Saturday Night Live (with Aerosmith). I was sitting in the stands with Rita Wilson.

Chris Farley in our weight room, after a game, wearing my jersey. Chris Chelios said, "That may be the first time that jersey's had sweat in it."

Sunday racing at my "Weekend at Bernie's" charity weekend. David Wells, Jeremy Roenick, me, and Kurt Busch.

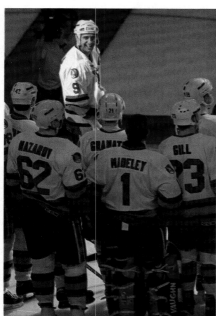

Surrounded by my Sharks teammates, celebrating my 1,000th NHL game on Saturday night, November 2, 1996. *(Paul Sakuma/AP Images)*

My last year in the league. *(Ian Tomlinson /Allsport/ Getty Images)*

Me and a friend's daughter with gold-medalist Amanda Kessel at Wayne Gretzky's fantasy camp.

Drew Doughty and me when I was coaching with the Kings.

Los Angeles Kings Legends Night in 2011 with my daughter McKenna. *(Noah Graham/NHLI via Getty Images)*

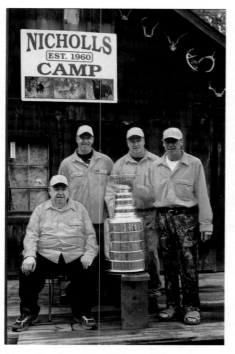

At our family camp with my dad
and two brothers.

With the Cup in my canoe that
my dad made for me.

The Cup with my mom and Uncle Lyle.

Me and McKenna with the Cup.

With McKenna on the ice
after the Kings won the Cup.

June 11, 2012: Standing on the ice, holding up the Stanley Cup. *(Bruce Bennett/ Getty Images)*

"No, I think it just went in the rough," Peter would answer. Once he would get up near where his ball should be, it would miraculously reappear.

"Here it is!"

I love golf, but I don't fool myself about how good I am. There are so many guys on the lower tours. They can go out and shoot 66, 67 and anybody can do that. But to do it every day like the big boys do? We used to have a celebrity tour. You could earn a little money. I played the stop in Tahoe for 10 years. Mike Eruzione and I were the first hockey players to play there.

There's a big difference between the feeling of a hockey game and playing golf. I could play on the ice in front of 18,000–20,000 fans and I was fine. When I tee the ball up, there's people around and it gets quiet. I don't like it when the crowd starts to get quiet.

"No, no, make noise, cheer," I say.

I'd rather have them yelling at me because I'm going to be more comfortable hitting the ball. And when there's people lining the fairways—not that I'm afraid I'm not going to hit it straight—but it's a little nerve-racking.

I found playing golf helped me relax. I would play golf in the play-offs all the time. You'd have your day off between games or between a series. To me that's a chance to go and get away. Chris Chelios wasn't a big golfer, but we'd still go out on our day off to get away from the rink. We'd ride in a cart. We were covered. It's not like we were in the sun, we weren't walking, and it was relaxing. Then the next day we were back at it.

In Chicago we played great courses—Medinah and Chicago Country Club to name a couple. New York had some unbelievable golf courses. There are so many beautiful courses up and down California. And I've probably played five or six U.S. Open golf courses.

I hate to admit it, but I was a club thrower. I've put a club through a cart or through the window before. Just stupid. One time I was playing in San Diego with Paul Ysebaert and Joe Murphy. Murph wasn't very good. He'd get frustrated pretty quick. In San Diego, he walked off the course in the middle of a round.

We had a good group in Chicago of maybe eight to 10 guys who would play. We played 3-putt. If you 3-putted a hole, you'd have to put your tee down. Last person to 3-putt had to pay everyone else.

In other words, if you 3-putt the 18th hole and nobody else in the group 3-putts, you have to pay off everyone who is playing. We usually agreed to a $20 ante on this game. If 10 golfers were in, you had to pay $180 if you were the last 3-putter.

People ask if I would consider playing professionally and absolutely I would. I remember the first time playing in San Jose. Someone took me up to the Olympic Club in San Francisco. I shot a 72, and someone said I should try to turn pro.

But those guys are good. I'm a 1-handicap, but PGA guys are a plus–4, plus–5, plus–6. You see the guys on the Nike Tour and it's no different than hockey people. Just because a player dominates in the American Hockey League doesn't mean he will dominate in the NHL. There's a big difference between the minors and the NHL.

And there's a big difference between being a 1-handicap and playing on the PGA tour.

CHAPTER 12

NOBODY EVER
BEATS THE HOUSE

DURING THE 1994–95 SEASON, Joe Murphy and I were betting on NFL games with a Chicago bookie. I was up $51,000 and Murphy was down $37,000.

The bookie wouldn't pay me until Murphy paid him. But Murphy had a different idea: he wanted to try to win his money back by betting on the NBA. I didn't know much about the NBA but I went along with it.

It didn't take us long to get caught up in NBA scores. Obviously, we bet on the Chicago Bulls because we knew the players. We always knew what was going on with that team because during Blackhawks games they would give you scores on the scoreboard.

One night, late in a game, during a TV timeout, it was kind of quiet on the bench when all of a sudden Murphy just screamed with delight. It was like he had just scored an overtime playoff goal.

Murphy had just seen the Bulls' final on the scoreboard and we had won our bet.

Even the referees looked over when Murphy screamed. Sutter didn't know what the fuck was going on. But I'm sure he found out later and probably wasn't thrilled about it. He would view that as us not being focused on the game. But that's really silly because when I'm on the ice I'm sure not thinking about what's happening in an NBA game.

But the Blackhawks played a bunch of Sunday games, and Murphy and I had the trainer or a player not in the lineup informing us of what was happening with the games we had bet on.

To be honest, keeping track of our NFL and NBA bets on Sunday was a bit of a distraction.

However, I can tell you that Murphy and I were not the only NHL players betting on games in the 1990s. There were a lot more players betting on football than anyone realized. Sometimes, it would be guys that you least suspect who were betting.

I played with Tony Granato later in my career, and it surprised me that he would lay a few bucks on an NFL game.

At that time, call-in tip lines were popular with players. I had a team-mate in New Jersey who liked one specific line. I remember he called it and the tipster made a prediction on what was going to happen in that game that night. He said one team was going to be down and then there was going to be a turnover near the end of the half and then the other team was going to dominate in the second and win.

That's exactly what happened in the game. He was an unbelievable teammate, but he was sold on this tipster. He ended up pouring a lot of money into this guy and he didn't deliver like he did on his first prognostication. He won a few games with the guy, but eventually it went south on him. At one point, the Devils started giving his paychecks to his wife. I felt bad because he is such a stand-up guy. Lamoriello loved him.

I started gambling almost the first day I showed up in Los Angeles. I don't recall exactly, but it seems like I was going to the track the first week I was there. Horses. Poker. Betting on the NFL. Casinos. And shooting craps is my favorite.

One time, I was shooting craps in Las Vegas and my sister Alberta was standing behind me. I was so hot that I won about $8,000. But I was also handing a $100 black chip to Alberta every time I won. She was surprised to have $2,100 when I was done with my run.

I played in a charity gambling tournament in Atlantic City with former major league pitcher Tug McGraw years ago and there was a guy in our group who was a professional gambler. His game was craps. I told him I'd always wanted to learn to play.

"Come on down tonight and I will teach you how to play," the guy said.

That night, he held the dice for 45 minutes and won more than $200,000. He taught me the game. He basically taught me to make only three kinds of bets, all based on the idea of maximizing your odds on every bet.

I love craps because it feels like when you understand the game you have better odds of winning than you have in other casino games.

Just because I know craps doesn't mean I win all the time. The most I ever won in one night at a casino was $10,000, and I gave that to my father. I just told him I won it and I wanted him to have it. I got more joy out of that than if I would have by buying something for me.

What did I need?

But my dad was as responsible for my career as I was. He taught me everything. George Nicholls was a truck driver who didn't work in the winter. He would trap to get through the winter. That $10,000 probably made it easier for my dad to pay the bills in the winter.

The most I ever lost in one night was $5,000 at a casino.

My biggest horse racing win was also $10,000. I won it betting on Barbaro in the 2006 Kentucky Derby. That's the horse that shattered his leg two weeks later at the Preakness. That injury eventually led to his death nine months later.

I tried to keep my betting reasonable. As I previously mentioned, gambling for me is more about the competition than the money. I want to beat you more than I want your money. I played plenty of Texas Hold 'Em games and the biggest buy-in I ever played was $1,000.

Never did I lose sight of the reality that you never win in the long run when you gamble. I'm sure I lost more than I won when I was gambling. In fact, I've never really met anyone who won more than they lost. How many times do you bet and lose and tell yourself there is no way I should have lost that bet? It never evens out. More bad than good happens to you when you bet.

No one is building those billion-dollar casinos in Las Vegas from the winnings of all the gamblers.

The story that started this chapter with me winning $51,000 on NFL games didn't have a happy ending. When Murphy and I were done betting on basketball, I owed $50,000. It was a $100,000 swing. I can tell you that there is nothing worse on a Tuesday morning than meeting with your bookie with an envelope full of hundred bills. After that bad experience, I never bet with a bookie again.

CHAPTER 13

SHARKS, SUTTERS, AND ONE DEAD COW

IN MY FIRST SEASON with the San Jose Sharks, I put up 45 points and I shot a cow. A guy who fancies himself an elite hunter, and an excellent shot, took aim and brought down a 1,200-pound farm animal.

As you can imagine, I've never been able to live that down.

Young Sharks forward Owen Nolan and I became instant friends when I arrived in San Jose. We often golfed and hunted together. One day, we hunted on a large parcel of land that Owen owned up in the hills. As daylight began slipping away, Owen spotted three or four bucks running up a hill. I climbed up for a better look and saw the group standing on the top of an adjacent hill. They might have been 100 yards away.

I fired and one animal rolled down the hill into the ravine. Dark was setting in and it was decided we'd have to wait until morning to find my kill. Because Owen and I had a scheduled practice, another hunter we were with said he would come out in the morning.

When our friend showed up in practice, he delivered the news that I had slayed a cow, not a buck.

Owen could not have been more amused and he told everyone in Santa Clara County the story about how I had shot a farmer's cow, thinking I was downing a buck.

He had way too much fun with the retelling of the tale. Fucking Owen made it seem like I was standing 20 feet from the cow when I shot it. He never mentioned it was dark.

At one point, he went out and purchased seat covers for my truck that had cows on them.

You wouldn't believe how quickly the story of my murdered cow made its way around the National Hockey League. I'd be lining up for a faceoff and my opponent would say, "Hey, I heard you shot a cow."

Everyone had plenty of fun at my expense. It's been 25 years and still to this day, people remind me of the day I bagged a cow.

One person I never told about the cow was my dad. He had raised me to be prideful and certainly to be a skilled hunter. No one could shoot as accurately as my dad could, but I think he thought I was close.

One time we were hunting for moose in Quebec, and I went off by myself. I brought down a moose. When I called him on the cell, he said he already knew.

"I heard the shot," he said.

That was a proud moment for me because it was Dad saying he knew if I shot, I wasn't going to miss.

That's why I didn't tell him that I killed a cow.

In my first season with the Sharks, I definitely thought I made the right decision to sign with the team. They brought in veteran players Tony Granato, Marty McSorley, Al Iafrate, and Todd Gill. The Sharks already had quality youngsters, such as Owen Nolan, Jeff Friesen, Viktor Kozlov, Marcus Ragnarsson, and Mike Rathje.

We had the makings of a quality team. But the Sharks had a hole behind the bench. The Sharks had missed the boat on the decision to hire rookie coach Al Sims.

But even though I knew immediately we had the wrong coach, I was very happy from the beginning in San Jose. My wife and children joined me in Northern California after staying in Southern California when I played in Chicago.

Plus, I had my agreement with Dean Lombardi about what my role would be. I would start out in a scoring role and then transition into becoming a bottom-six forward with my main duty being mentoring the younger players.

I wanted to play until I was 40, and the Lombardi plan seemed like it would allow me to accomplish that objective.

When it comes to the regular season and playoffs, I always said a good start was important to having a quality season or a productive postseason. In my first game with the Sharks in 1996–97, I scored a goal and added an assist when we tied the New York Islanders on opening night. The next night I had four points against the Kings in Los Angeles.

In my first training camp, Sims put me with Owen Nolan. I immediately tried to get close with him. But he was different from friends and linemates I'd had in the past. He was a lot different.

He was challenging to play with because he was just a different player. He was a great player. He was just difficult to read.

That first year, if we were doing a drill, and someone missed a pass to him, he might have a funny reaction. With the next guy up, Owen would just shoot the puck into the corner. Like, "Hey, I didn't make the bad pass, he did."

The Sharks had acquired him on October 26, 1995, for Sandis Ozoliņš, who turned into the final piece of a Stanley Cup championship for the Avalanche.

I always said if Owen played Colorado 80 times a year, he'd score 60 goals. He would get fired up to play against the Avalanche because they didn't want him. They chose to trade him. Owen had a burr up his ass about missing out on that championship run. He had been a member of their young corps and they went and won without him. That's why he loved going back to Colorado and having a big night.

When Owen wanted to play? Oh my! He was a bull in a china shop—a pure power forward. I knew coming to San Jose that's who I was going to play with, at least initially. Owen was the best player, so I just had to bond with him, try to get to know him, and learn from him.

I bought a place at Silver Creek Country Club four houses from the clubhouse. And Owen had a place on the hill above me. So, I spent a lot of time with Owen. We both lived in the same area, so we golfed and hunted together.

I took Owen to Vegas that first year. It was Mike Tyson's first fight since getting out of prison. I bought two tickets: $1,500 apiece. And in 89 seconds the fight was over. Iron Mike knocked Peter McNeeley out. "Holy shit!" Three thousand dollars for the tickets, and we weren't even there for two minutes!

Owen and I roomed together on the road for a while, and he'd just signed for $30 million over six years. If you don't pay your room bill, the team will deduct it off your check. We're in Anaheim and we had a bill for $6. It was mine, and I didn't pay for it. When we came down to check out, he lost his mind over $6! He said, "I ain't paying it!"

That was him. He was just a young kid.

Sims just didn't seem to know how to turn us around. He was a highly regarded assistant on Ron Wilson's coaching staff in Anaheim, and Dean Lombardi gave him his first chance to be an NHL head coach.

Our game-day practices were 45 minutes to an hour long sometimes, and they were hard. As older players we had to go tell him we couldn't do that. Some guys wouldn't even go on the ice. They'd tell the trainers they were hurt even if they weren't. I broke my thumb early in the season, and I had something later, too, and it was because he worked the guys too much. We were on the ice way too much. We were always worn out.

Hiring Sims was a bad decision because even if you are bringing in older players to create leadership you also need direction from the coach. You need a coach making sure everyone is on the same page. And we didn't have that.

By Christmas time we knew Sims had to go. I was at the team party. It was the first time in my career players and coaches were at the same holiday party. I know Dean was there, too. We were only 30 games into the season, but Dean came away knowing he had to fire the coach. Everyone was talking about it. It was too late already.

I was friends with team president Greg Jamison, who later had a piece of team ownership. We talked about a replacement coach. I suggested two names: Darryl Sutter and Jacques Lemaire. And Greg talked to them because Jacques called to thank me for bringing his name up. I know Greg listened.

This team had loads of potential. I got to know Owen Nolan well and he was a talented player. He was 24 when I arrived in San Jose and Owen already had four seasons of scoring 30 or more goals. I felt Owen needed a veteran coach to handle him effectively. Owen was too much for an inexperienced coach. I made it perfectly clear to Greg that we needed Darryl Sutter. He could handle Owen's personality. I told Greg he'd be making a mistake if he didn't hire Darryl.

And that's what happened in the offseason.

Another time Owen wanted to borrow my gun. I bought a brand-new, 7mm rifle to hunt. He had a buddy visiting who wanted to borrow it. No problem. When Owen dropped it off, I opened the case and saw the gun was all scratched. Someone either fell or something, and Owen didn't tell me.

That first season, you want to get off to a good start for your new team. You come with a bunch of new guys, and you want to get off on the right foot. We had some real character veterans: Bob Errey, Tim Hunter, Todd Ewen, Ed Belfour, and Kelly Hrudey.

And how about this? The tough guys have such a hard job. In training camp, Tim and Todd had to warm up, I guess. Right there in training camp they went at it. Why wouldn't you wait for an exhibition game? Instead you're fighting amongst yourselves!

We had a great group of guys, and two great goalies. For me, the great thing about the game is everyone you meet. We had a great group of older guys, a great mixture of younger guys. We were set up to be successful. We had the making of a pretty good team.

I had one unexpected scare during that season. I ended up having polyps in my bladder. I was pissing blood. I went to Stanford, and they took the polyps out. A Stanford doctor said he was 95 percent sure it was cancer. I had to wait a week to find out what it was, and I didn't say anything to anybody. I told my mum I pulled my groin. It turned out it wasn't cancer, it was just the polyps growing in there. Why would you ever say that to somebody?

Older players need to be good leaders, work hard, and help the kids. I can't think of any veterans they brought in who didn't get along with everybody. I'd broken my ankle a few games earlier and played my last game on March 11. There were still 15 games left. Toward the end of me trying to play, they'd freeze my ankle. I wouldn't practice, but I would play.

There were a few rumors in the offseason the Sharks were interested in Gretz. He'd finished the year playing for St. Louis and he was a free agent. Who wouldn't at least make a phone call to his agent?

Dean might have let it slip out, or someone might have said something for the fans that we were trying to get Gretzky. We did hear that. But Gretz never mentioned it or talked about it to me. I only remember hearing the Sharks talking about it.

That would have been a pretty good opportunity for the organization to have him there for one or two years. New York or San Jose? It was a pretty easy decision for Gretz, right? He signed with the Rangers and finished his career in the Big Apple.

After the season ended and Sims was let go, I knew Darryl Sutter was who the Sharks were going after. Knowing how much Darryl loves the game, loves hockey, and just wanted to be a part of it, I figured there would be no doubt he'd be there. Darryl had stepped away from the Blackhawks a couple years earlier to spend more time on the family farm in Viking, Alberta. He was ready to come back.

Hockey is a passion for Darryl. And with his youngest son, Chris, Darryl knew Chris loved hockey, too. To be able to bring him along to San Jose was perfect. I was happy. I loved playing for Darryl. I really enjoy him as a person. I just knew it was the right time and he was the right guy for any team.

Darryl gets the best out of everybody. I thought he'd be perfect for Owen because Darryl is a no-bullshit kind of a guy. Darryl loves the older players, too, and we had a good group of veterans. I was definitely excited when Darryl came.

We didn't get off to the fastest start. We were eight games under .500 after two months and knew there was a lot of work ahead to get where we wanted to go. But I think we knew we had the players to do it.

I'd broken my thumb in Anaheim on November 10, and it was hunting season back home. I told our trainer, Ray Tufts, he had to tell Darryl that the doctor wanted me to take a week off and didn't want me skating or doing anything.

Darryl knew why. He knew me, knew my family. So, he said yes, and I went home hunting with my dad for a week. I managed to do that twice in my career!

I played a little bit with Tony Granato, with Owen early on, and with Murray Craven later, too. We added some toughness and real quality guys as the season progressed. Bryan Marchment, Dave Lowry, Mike Ricci, Johnny MacLean, Stéph Matteau, Murph, and Mike Vernon were all added. Eddie Belfour had left, but we still had two great goalies.

That was also the season when NHL players participated in the Olympics for the first time. We had 17 days off in February before we played again. Some of us went to Hawaii, including Joe Murphy and me.

Someone opened a roller rink on the beach, that was cool. And Randy Morton put us up at the Four Seasons in Maui for 10 days. What a great break for us during the season. Then when we came back, Darryl took us up to Banff—a ski resort near Calgary—for the team to get back into it.

It was a great time for all the veterans to mix with the younger guys and really bond. Us older guys were pretty much all the same age. I remember Murray Craven was a great skier. I was nervous because I was just an average skier. Murray would just fly down the slopes.

So, we were in Hawaii for 10 days—golfing and just hanging out—and then we went to Banff to hold a mini training camp. When we got to playing, between the rest the veterans got and the team bonding after, we really took off and made a nice run.

We played a lot of 3–2, 2–1 hockey games. It was Sutter hockey, and he loved it.

Late in the season, we played a game against the Rangers at Madison Square Garden that meant a lot to us. The Rangers scored three power play goals and beat us 5–3. I thought referee Don Koharski screwed us.

My postgame rant made all the newspapers and caught the attention of the league office.

The reason I was incensed is that Koharski decided to crack down on obstruction by calling two ticky-tack penalties against us. That resulted in the Rangers gaining a five-on-three power play. They scored twice in about 30 seconds.

Koharski only called those penalties because the league had sent around a memo saying they wanted obstruction called tighter heading into the playoffs.

A month before, maybe even a week before, those penalties would not have been called.

"If that's what Brian Burke wants, or [Gary] Bettman, they have a serious problem. That gave them all the momentum, right here in New York, where Brian Burke is. If he likes that, then he's got a big problem. There were two really questionable calls that at the first of the year wouldn't have been called, period, let alone to put a team on a five-on-three. That's unbelievable."

I wasn't done, not even close.

"If that's what the league wants, that's why our league is going backward. The wrong people...they don't understand what makes our game go. They want to make changes. Changes? Well, change the people who are running it. That's B.S. That's about all I've got to say about that."

What the papers couldn't print was all the f-bombs in my quotes. I must have said "fuck" or "fucking" 10 times. In the cramped press room afterward, I was told a wire service reporter was overheard telling editors his story was late because "he had to take all the 'fucks' out of his story before he could file it."

When we interviewed Burke for this book, he recalled that Bettman told him to "fine the piss out of Bernie."

Bettman's position was that the league couldn't tolerate players badmouthing the officials because it undermined their authority.

It helped that I called and apologized to Burke and Koharski. Burke decided he wasn't going to fine me. But first he called Koharski to make sure he was okay with that.

"All the referees liked Bernie," Burke said in the telling of this story.

Burke did give me a conditional fine, which he said he did when he felt the player deserved a break.

"Look, I've never had a problem with you and I'm not giving you a fine. But I'll collect $20,000 from you if we have another incident in the next 18 months."

Early in my career, referees gave me a lot of 10-minute misconducts because I chirped all the time. But then I grew up, matured a little bit, and got along great with officials. I always talked to the referee and linesman during the game. And they would let me know if they thought I was getting out of hand.

One night, Bob Hodges grew tired of hearing my complaints. On a faceoff, he let me know how he felt.

"You are never going to win another faceoff," he said.

He threw the puck right between my legs. I thought it was awesome. He made his point.

You can't blame them. They take so much abuse. They don't deserve it. Referees don't cheat. They miss calls from time to time. But most of the time, they do their best and do a good job. When I realized that, I started to become friends with them.

It takes time, and we had a lot of new players. Darryl was trying to get a feel for who fit with whom because we had the makings of a good team. We had two great goalies, some skill, strong defense, and plenty of new faces. It just took a little while for everyone to gel with one another.

With Darryl, he looked at our team like it was a wild stallion. He had to break us down and break us in before he could ride us. Once he did that, we finished strong, climbed our way into eighth place and into the playoffs. That was an impressive accomplishment considering the team had finished last for two seasons.

We played a great team in Dallas to start the playoffs. They'd won the Central Division and we were fourth in the Pacific—1 vs. 8 in the conference. The Stars won the first two games at home, but we rallied at the Shark Tank to tie the series.

We won Game 4 in dramatic fashion: 1–0 in overtime. Rookie defenseman Andrei Zyuzin, just a 20-year-old kid, scored to win it. And I set him up. I came around from behind the net as he snuck in. I hit him with a pass, and he let 'er rip. People still talk to this day about how loud that building gets. During playoff time the Shark Tank is as loud as any arena in the league.

Some buildings are just always loud, and that one is. Playoff hockey is cool to play in, especially there. It's so loud when you skate through the Shark Head. Other teams have tried something similar, but credit who came up with the Shark Head.

Dallas was the best team in the conference, and we were staying right with them. We knew we had a good team; we just ran into the best team, or we might have been able to do a little something. As it was, Dallas won the next two games and ended the series in six.

The next season, which ended up being my last, we held training camp in San Jose and opened in Japan with two games against Calgary. Hanging out in Japan with Murph was memorable. We just hammered the sushi. It was a lot of fun opening the season there.

We played in what had been an indoor swimming venue at one time. You could smell chlorine and there was a diving board near one end of the rink. It was one of the first times the league sent teams overseas to play regular season games.

My career ended abruptly. No warning. No tearful announcement. No final game to share with my friends and family. We had just played a 2–2 tie against Wayne Gretzky's New York Rangers on November 21, 1998. Lombardi called me into the office. It was a short meeting. He said he was removing me from the roster. Lombardi still had to pay me, so Darryl asked if I could stay with the organization as an assistant coach. He knew I could be a good buffer between the coaches and players.

Eighteen years in the NHL. A total of 1,127 regular season games. And it was all over in 90 seconds.

I was in shock, dumbfounded by what I had been just told.

Lombardi asked me if I wanted him to explore trade options. But that wasn't going to work. It was early in the season and most general managers had their teams the way they wanted them. I didn't think there would be a strong market for me. But more importantly, one reason why I picked San Jose was the opportunity to be back with my children. I didn't want to leave them again after finally getting back together.

Bottom line: Another promise made to me that had been broken. Bruce McNall and Neil Smith promised not to trade me and did. Now, Lombardi was not honoring his word about my role in the third season.

I'm sure Lombardi saw the situation differently, but that was my view on what unfolded in San Jose.

So much was wrong with the way my career ended. My plan was to play until I was 40 and I fell short of that. I was 37 when I was tossed overboard. I was also 25 goals short of 500. If I played until I was 40, maybe I would have made it. Maybe not. I had no goals in my first 10 games that season.

The worst part of the situation was the fact that there was no closure. I didn't know it was coming. Had I been given warning, I would have had my parents come in, invited some important people in my life. I would have claimed a few mementos from the game as souvenirs. Felt like I deserved a better goodbye.

Whatever happened to the idea that your word is your bond in hockey?

The Sharks had drafted Patrick Marleau the summer before, and they had asked me to work with him. That fit into what Lombardi had talked to me about when I signed. I was doing that, working with Patrick every chance I got.

But the situation had changed. Darryl had brought in his brother Ron and Dave Lowry to play on the fourth line.

"I want Ronnie as the fourth line center," he told Lombardi.

I get it. If I were the coach, I'd take my brother, too. But it was up to Lombardi to say no to Darryl.

He should have told Darryl that he had a handshake deal in place with me about what my role was going to be. The truth was I was also better for that role than Ron was. I had more things to offer.

We had already agreed on that. And that's what pissed me off about Dean. He had no courage to stand up to Darryl. Dean apologized to me a year or two later saying he did the wrong thing. I told him, "You just didn't have the balls."

Again, I am sure Lombardi would have a different perspective, but from where I was sitting, Darryl ran the team. He and Dean fought all the time. Darryl's been a general manager. He's been a coach. He knows both sides of it. He pretty much wanted it his way. Going into it, Dean was supposed to do what he was supposed to do, and he didn't. It bothers me to this day because it shouldn't have ended the way it did. When you don't keep your word, it stings a little bit.

CHAPTER 14

FIGHT CLUB

HOW'S THAT SONG GO? You don't tug on Superman's cape. You don't spit into the wind. You don't pull the mask off the ol' Lone Ranger and don't mess around with fucking Wayne Gretzky.

Something like that.

I learned the hard way it was hazardous to my health to touch Gretzky during an NHL game in his days with the Edmonton Oilers.

The first time I played for the Los Angeles Kings against Gretzky a fight started. I grabbed Gretz because that's what everybody did when there was a fight in an NHL game. You found a partner to make sure no one was free to jump into the fray. Non-fighters paired off and waited for everything to cool off.

But as soon as I had a good grip on Wayne, defenseman Lee Fogolin and another Oiler were in my face.

"Don't fucking touch him," Fogolin said.

If I could have foreseen the future, I would have said, "Don't worry guys, a few years from now I'll be eating lunch at McDonalds with Wayne three times a week and hanging with him on the road."

Instead, I said, "Oh, shit. Okay, no problem."

Chalk that mistake up to a young player not knowing any better. Today, fighting has been reduced dramatically in the NHL. But when

I played, especially early in my career, it was part of the strategy that teams employed to win. Fighting was tied into the sport's culture.

The "tough guy" role was just one of the jobs on an NHL team. Some guys score, some play strong defense, and one, sometimes two guys were signed to fight. Every team had a tough guy and their role was to protect their teammates. They all took their job seriously.

When Ken Baumgartner protected us in Los Angeles in the late 1980s, he was good at this job. He was always with me. He used to walk into the Kings dressing room and say loudly, "Daddy's home!"

Baumgartner was such a smart guy. In the offseason, he took college classes. It took him 14 years, but he ended up with a degree in business and finance from Hofstra University on Long Island. Then he went to Harvard and started to work on his MBA. If you met him outside of hockey, it wouldn't occur to you that he would be making his living as an enforcer.

I remember there were four or five brawls in a game against the Philadelphia Flyers, and he didn't fight. We were walking out of the rink together. Back then, we would park right out front of the Forum so when it was time to leave, our cars were close to the exit. As we exited the arena, a fan started coming toward us. He was chirping at me, commenting on what I did or didn't do in the game. He had complaints, fueled by alcohol.

Kenny stepped in, and then the guy started chirping at Kenny. Either the guy took a swing at Kenny, pushed him, or both. I don't remember specifically what started the fight. But I do recall Kenny finished it like he was Mike Tyson.

But after this so-called fan made the first move, Kenny beat the hell out of him. Kenny had him down and was punching him against the cement. Luckily for us, an undercover cop saw it all play out. He knew the fan had started it. Kenny was just defending himself. I don't know what the fan was thinking. I don't think he intended to tangle with

Kenny. The drinking probably clouded his judgment. But he picked the wrong guy to fight that night.

Back then, players interacted with players regularly. But that is the only instance I can remember of a player fighting with a fan.

The game was different back then. It was definitely tough, often chippy, and sometimes dirty. Fighting was just part of our routine.

Even if you were a skilled player, you had to drop the gloves sometimes. After my career ended, I was asked to guess the number of fights I had. My guess was eight or nine? Turns out I had 23 fighting majors and there were four other times, including one in the postseason, when my "opponent" was given five minutes while I got away with either a minor or no penalty at all!

I didn't often fight toe-to-toe. That definitely was not my style. I probably could have since I have pretty long arms and I am quick. But I was afraid if I stood in and traded punches with a skilled fighter, I would be on the losing end too often. That's why my usual strategy was to get inside the other guy and hold on. It was more like wrestling matches than a traditional hockey fight.

My first career fight was late in the 1981–82 season after I was called up by the Kings. I squared off in the third period against Bob Lorimer of the Colorado Rockies. He was a 28-year-old defenseman, and I was 20 and too inexperienced to know what I was getting into.

Two of my fighting majors were in the playoffs. The first one was early in the third period of the "Miracle on Manchester" when we rallied from a 5–0 deficit in Game 3 against the Oilers to win in overtime. I fought Dave Lumley. That fucking guy. He was all over me, and I took the bait. I shouldn't have been taking dumb penalties with him. That was not a good trade for our team.

I missed almost the entire third period and just enough of OT to still be in the box when Daryl Evans scored the winner.

During the 1984–85 playoffs I remember being on the ice between the benches at Edmonton. I paired off with Oilers defenseman Larry

Melnyk in the middle of a big scrum. He was a year older and maybe 10–15 pounds heavier. I hit Larry, and he hit me. All of a sudden, Larry wasn't doing anything. And I'm just reefing him with shots to the head and he's not hitting me back.

I'm thinking, *What the fuck is going on here? You started this fight!*

Turns out my teammate big Brian MacLellan had a bear hug on Larry. He couldn't move, even though I was punching him in the head. It was kind of a one-sided fight because Larry had both of his hands tied. I'm friends with Larry now, and we've done hockey-related charity events and appearances together since retiring. I scored later to tie it, but the Oilers won in OT.

The Oilers not only went on to sweep the series but lost only three times the rest of the way to win its second straight Stanley Cup.

When anger gets the best of you, poor decisions are made, especially when you are a young player.

One time in Los Angeles, early in my career, I was tangled up with a player—I don't even remember who it was. But I know he ended up with his fingers in my mouth.

My reaction was to bite down like I was trying to rip them off.

Blood began to flow, and my opponent screamed like he was in a horror movie.

"He bit me. He bit me," he yelled at the referee.

The referee looked straight at me.

"Did you bite him?" he asked.

"No, I didn't bite him. I don't know what he's talking about," I said, with his blood dripping from my lips.

When it came to physical play and fighting, I played smarter as I got more experienced. For one thing, I'd keep my stick in my hands instead of dropping it.

We used to play Vancouver like 12 times a year because we'd train near them and then play them all the time in our division. We had some nasty fights in training camp.

I had a bad habit of drawing misconducts at the end of games, just from running my mouth at the opposition. There's not a worse penalty in the world than a yapping penalty. You get 10 minutes for just being out of control.

Never did I go looking for a fight, but I didn't mind being in them.

I just didn't want to get hit in the head. But if someone came after me, I defended myself.

When Dale Hawerchuk played for the Buffalo Sabres, he beat my ass one night. I elbowed Alexander Mogilny in the head. It was kind of dirty. Dale jumped me and took care of me quickly.

That wasn't my dirtiest play. Once, when I was playing against the Colorado Avalanche, I butt-ended Adam Deadmarsh. We were skating, and he was right behind me. I'm not sure he was doing anything to me. Or I don't remember if he was.

For whatever reason, I took one hand off my stick and butt-ended him hard. He punched me in the back of the head and dropped me.

I looked up and said, "Good enough. I deserved that."

I actually started laughing because he got his revenge immediately. He didn't need to do anything else because he nailed me in the back of the head so hard. He got me good. I don't even think he got a penalty. There was only one referee at the time, and he couldn't see everything.

I certainly tried to stand up for my teammates. When Calgary defenseman Rob Ramage punched Mike Murphy hard enough to spin his Jofa helmet right off his head, I immediately went after Ramage.

My slash was vicious enough to earn a major penalty.

Rob was a big, strong boy. I'm not sure what I was thinking there. I might have been holding on for dear life.

I remember a close call with Tim Hunter in Calgary. Marty McSorley started a melee. Marty was being Marty, pounding the shit out of Theo Fleury all night. That triggered a brawl. Everyone paired off. Hunter grabbed my jersey. As we drifted way off to the side, he pulled me down.

The referee came over and said, "Tim, don't hit him."

"No, no, I'm not gonna." Hunter said.

I didn't like the look in Hunter's eye.

"Don't you fucking leave!" I yelled to the referee.

If the referee left, I was sure Hunter would have pounded me.

Not sure why I became involved in so many skirmishes in the NHL, because I was not a fighter in junior hockey. Not at all.

But at the NHL level, my mouth got me in trouble more than once. I was always talking to someone on the ice.

If the opposing goalie would make a quality save against us, I would tap the goalie on the pads and say, "Good save."

Goalies didn't know how to react to that. But I can tell you that some of them absolutely hated it.

Another one of my moves was to carry on a dialogue with a defenseman and then run him over. They just never expected me to run them over. Some would get angry to be sure.

I had five scraps in 1986–87, and four other times the guy I was mixing it up with got a fighting major while I skated free with a minor or nothing at all! Five came in a five-game span that ended right before Christmas.

I fought Kelly Kisio of the Rangers first, though I received only a roughing minor while he was assessed five for fighting. Two games later, in Edmonton, Raimo Summanen and I exchanged spears, dropped 'em, and he turtled.

A couple games later in Calgary, I met up with Mike Bullard twice the same night, though I was assessed only one major. The last one was against Jim Benning, who kind of suckered me.

The season before, I fought Marc Crawford, who of course later became a coach in the NHL. I never liked him, and still don't. I don't remember much about it other than I probably enjoyed it.

And I fought Gary Lupul later the same night. Another one that season was with Ray Ferraro. There's one where two guys who don't really fight squared off. Ray could be a little mouthy. He probably said or did something to tick me off. Fighting Ray was fun, fighting Bullard was fun.

But fighting Ramage and a couple of those other guys, well, I needed to be careful. A non-fighter can get himself in trouble fighting someone who knows what they are doing.

Speaking of fighting tough guys, I'll never forget big defenseman Jim Kyte showing a lot of self-control. A fight had started, and Jimmy grabbed me. He was holding me and from the bench Dan Maloney (the coach!) was yelling, "Fucking hit him!"

He was yelling at Jimmy to hit me, and Jimmy wouldn't. We had our gloves off and we were just holding on. Thank God Jimmy didn't hit me. I was happy about that.

In 1983–84 I had three fights: Brian Bellows, Phil Housley, and Kevin Lowe. Phil threw 'em pretty good. Kevin could be a dirty prick, too. It was just us being hockey players. We could be chippy. And we played Edmonton all the time.

Of course, Kevin and I became friends when he was captain of the Oilers and I joined them later. I had five fights in my real rookie season of 1982–83: Dale Hawerchuk, Mike Antonovich, Wally Weir, and Tim Watters twice (different games). Sometimes you get tested as a new player, not really a surprise back then. Dale was tough. He beat my ass after I elbowed one of his teammates in the head. It was kind of dirty. Dale jumped me and took care of me quickly.

You always remember guys like that. I remember Watters. He was pretty dirty toward me. Wally Weir was a pretty big guy. Late during my time with the Kings, I fought Randy Carlyle. I don't know if this was before or after, but we were playing in the 'Peg. There was a big ruckus in the corner, like three or four guys in there, and I'm in the slot. I yell out, "Kitty!" And he fires the puck right to me, I deked the goalie, and Randy came skating in hard to try to cover the net. He was too late—I scored, and he ended up hurting his knee after crashing into the net. He got carried off and I saw him afterward on crutches. He was embarrassed that he set me up for a goal, then tore up his knee.

I was suspended a handful of times in my career. The first time was because of Ulf Samuelsson, who was a pain-in-the-ass defenseman for 16 seasons. He did something, so I turned, swung my stick, and hit him right in the head. I got five games for that in March of 1988. It was an accident all right. An accident on purpose! There was a defenseman in Montreal—can't recall his name—who wanted to fight me, but I had a separated shoulder. I got my stick up, and I sort of just whacked him with my stick on his hands. Got suspended for that. There was a time when you could get suspended, but not miss games.

The punishment was "days" so I could play games, but not practice. I was with the Devils and I got 14 days! I remember the bus came to pick us up at the team hotel for a practice and a limo came right behind it.

The team bus went to the practice rink, and the limo took me to a golf course in Florida! They got rid of that rule in a hurry because guys were getting suspended all the time. I remember a game while playing with San Jose when Florida defenseman Ed Jovanovski was all over Tony Granato all night. He had Tony down and I came over and cross-checked him in the face—split him wide open and was suspended two games for my action.

Tony played a little outside the lines. He would chirp at guys. I don't know what he did, or said, to Ed. But he angered the big fellow. I figured he would be looking to even the score against me.

Next time we played Florida, later that season, I was thinking I'd absolutely be killed. And the whole night Jovo Cop didn't do anything to me. He paid no attention to me at all. Instead, he was after Tony again. Thank God!

Bernie Nicholls Career Fight Card

No.	Date	Opponent	Period
1.	Mar. 27, 1982	Bob Lorimer, Colorado Rockies	13:59 2nd
2.	Apr. 10, 1982 *	Dave Lumley, Edmonton Oilers	2:23 3rd
3.	Dec. 29, 1982	Dale Hawerchuk, Winnipeg Jets	13:28 3rd
4.	Jan. 16, 1983	Mike Antonovich, New Jersey Devils	9:05 3rd
5.	Mar. 13, 1983	Tim Watters Winnipeg Jets	11:47 1st
6.	Ma. 24, 1983	Wally Weir, Quebec Nordiques	18:30 1st
7.	Mar. 30, 1983	Tim Watters, Winnipeg Jets	6:52 2nd
8.	Oct. 5, 1983	Brian Bellows, Minnesota North Stars	3:55 OT
9.	Oct. 28, 1983	Phil Housley, Buffalo Sabres	17:18 2nd
10.	Mar. 31, 1984	Kevin Lowe, Edmonton Oilers	18:44 3rd
11.	Mar. 10, 1985	Brent Peterson, Buffalo Sabres	7:08 3rd
12.	Apr. 10, 1985 *	Larry Melnyk, Edmonton Oilers	3:03 3rd
13.	Jan. 18, 1986	Marc Crawford, Vancouver Canucks	15:17 1st
14.	Jan. 18, 1986	Gary Lupul, Vancouver Canucks	13:08 3rd
15.	Mar. 22, 1986	Ray Ferraro, Hartford Whalers	18:10 3rd
16.	Dec. 14, 1986	Raimo Summanen, Edmonton Oilers	14:59 2nd
17.	Dec. 22, 1986	Mike Bullard, Calgary Flames	7:17 3rd
18.	Dec. 23, 1986	Jim Benning, Vancouver Canucks	16:32 2nd
19.	Feb. 16, 1987	Dan Daoust, Toronto Maple Leafs	8:19 1st
20.	Feb. 28, 1987	Chris Pryor, Minnesota North Stars	5:37 2nd
21.	Jan. 22, 1988	Randy Carlyle, Winnipeg Jets	20:00 3rd
22.	Jan. 30, 1988	Brian Lawton, Minnesota North Stars	11:49 1st
23.	Nov. 22, 1989	Mike Hudson, Chicago Blackhawks	17:38 2nd

*Playoffs

CHAPTER 15

TRYING TO BE MR. FIX-IT

MOST FOLKS IN THE HOCKEY WORLD don't know that I did earn a Stanley Cup championship ring, although it was not the way I thought I would earn it.

In about 2010, I turned into a fan of the Los Angeles Kings. It made sense: nine of my 18 seasons were spent in Los Angeles.

Watching games with an educated eye, I couldn't help but notice the Kings power play was dreadful. At the time, Terry Murray was the head coach. I saw problems with their approach and thought I could help turn them around.

First, I called general manager Dean Lombardi and told him I just wanted to help. I wasn't looking for a job. Honestly, I wasn't looking to take someone's job. Terry told me I couldn't be there just part-time: I'd have to be there all the time. He also was afraid I was looking at someone's job or something. Terry didn't think it would work out and Dean agreed so I let it go.

But the situation changed when the Kings fired Terry on December 12, 2011. After a 5–1–1 start, the Kings went 8–11–3. The team scored two or fewer goals in Murray's final eight games. In their first 29 games, the Kings had only scored 65 goals. Their power play was still ugly, and their morale and confidence were low.

The man entrusted to change all of that was Darryl Sutter. John Stevens kept the seat warm as interim coach until he could get there. Remember, I played for Darryl in Chicago and San Jose. He respected my abilities, even though he didn't always appreciate my attire, fondness for morning milkshakes, and my inability to put on a game face at 10:00 AM.

I called Darryl and told him I'd like to come and help his power play. I told him it had no direction. Darryl agreed and asked me to be in Los Angeles for 10:30 practice on January 3. The Kings were in a stretch of playing 10 of 13 games at home, making it an ideal opportunity to get plenty of practice time. That was critical in terms of teaching new ways of doing things. And it was awesome. I was going out with the guys every day.

After I started working with the Kings, we were shut out by Columbus the first game and the power play went 0-for-6. I thought, *Oh no!*

But we had a new director, and I was confident it would get better, even though we weren't seeing instant results.

When the homestand ended, I asked Darryl if he wanted me to go on the road with the team. He hadn't even taken a road trip with this team, and he said he wanted me on the trip.

I was all for that! We went to Calgary, Edmonton, and Vancouver. The results were win, a point in overtime, and win in a shootout. Great trip! I asked again what he wanted me to do.

"I want you to stay," Darryl said. Great! So next I went to Dean, but he wasn't in favor of it. Darryl was, and Darryl knew best anyways.

Dean called and put it something like, "I don't really want this, but Darryl does so let's sign it."

It was going good but we were still grinding because we weren't even in a playoff spot yet. I remember being on the ice, working with centermen on face-offs and other details, and telling them your power play doesn't always have to score, but it can't be a downer for the guys.

Even if you don't score on the power play, you have to create momentum or give us a spark. You have to produce scoring chances. If the power play is buzzing around the net, the team gets a lift.

This is what I felt: the Kings still weren't scoring as often as we should on the power play, but when we needed a power play goal, we could score it.

I promised Darryl.

We really started to build momentum after we acquired Jeff Carter from Columbus in late February. And we promoted a couple of kids: Dwight King and Jordan Nolan. And both were big boys. Between Carter and the call-ups, we added size and strength. I think Mike Richards was the smallest guy on the team and he was 5-foot-11, 195 pounds. Our goalie Jonathan Quick was amazing. He would later be MVP of the playoffs. And defenseman Drew Doughty was unbelievable.

Darryl would oversee the power play. I talked a lot of the x's and o's, worked on breakouts, suggested who should run a five-on-three, and just tried to give them direction and structure. It still wasn't great, but sometimes you can have all the best players on a power play and can't make it work. But it was definitely better.

One cool thing I remembered was how Darryl liked to operate from past experience. He could come in and just cut into the players. And the assistant coaches would walk out with him. Well, I had no problem staying behind and going up to guys and saying, "Look, it's not that bad."

I sometimes played the good cop to Darryl's bad cop.

After Darryl would harpoon someone, I could pat them on the butt and say, "Hey, Bud, here's what you're doing and here's what we're going to do."

I think that strategy worked exceptionally well with this team.

Darryl could be hard on players—not that they didn't deserve it, because most of the time they did. He made sure everyone was accountable. And he was tough on coaches, too. If you were not prepared, you were going to hear about it. I remember my first time going to the rink as a coach on a game day; I instantly realized the level of Darryl's preparation.

Darryl arrived by 4:00. And he'd quickly be pacing the floor. It was up to the other guys to stay on an even keel.

We couldn't have the players as tight and wound up as Darryl. He was intense from puck drop until the game was over. And he was awesome as long as we won. Lose and he could be tough. That was all right, too. The roughest line I heard from Darryl was one he gave us in San Jose.

"I hope everyone of you gets killed in an auto accident on the way home," Darryl said.

He was intense. That's the way he was. I was with the team the entire time. I think when I started, the idea was they'd want me to work with their kids in the American League. That's what Dean wanted. But Darryl wanted me there the entire time. It was such a dogfight the second half of the season just to qualify for the playoffs. Darryl wanted all hands on deck.

I think it was easier for players to relate to me instead of Darryl, or the other coaches, because they got along better with me. The remainder of that season was great. The team came together and played just so well to get in.

We went on a run (13–5–3) after Carter and the kids joined the lineup to finish third in the division and eighth in the conference. We were in San Jose for the last game of the regular season. If we won, we'd finish in seventh place and play St. Louis, which had the best home record. If we lost, we'd go to Vancouver, which had the most points in the league and won the Presidents' Trophy. Darryl asked the coaches, "Who do you want to play?"

Darryl never wanted to lose. I said I hoped we'd play Vancouver. Based on the times we'd played, I just thought we'd match up better against the Canucks than the Blues. And we ended up losing that last game to the Sharks in overtime. We went into Vancouver and swept the first two games. I think we shocked them. We were so big and physical, and Quick was so good. The Canucks had a great team and were expected to go a long way. But we manhandled them. Our special teams were good. Everything clicked. We went home and won Game 3. We lost Game 4 but went back into Vancouver and won Game 5 in overtime. I can still see Jarret Stoll scoring an unbelievable goal over Cory Schneider's shoulder to end the series right then and there. We went into St. Louis next and swept the first two there. But late in the second game, it got physical and out of hand.

The Blues were frustrated, and they had some big boys. We took some retaliatory penalties and a couple of fights. After the game Darryl snapped on the guys.

They had taken some dumb penalties because they were standing up for each other. Sutter hates dumb penalties.

Even though we killed off those penalties, Darryl tore into them. Then he walked out the room.

When I was just getting on the bus Darryl wasn't there yet. The three other coaches were. And I saw the boys were quiet in the back. I asked what was going on. And they told me what Darryl had said. I snapped on the coaches loud enough so the players in the back could all hear me.

"They just beat a team that lost nine games all season at home. They went in, stuck up for one another, and now they're back there with their heads between their legs feeling like they lost the first two games," I said.

I just went off on them.

"Yeah, you're right," Stevens, one of the assistants, said.

The players knew what they did. They killed the penalties, they'd learn from it, we needed to enjoy what we just did. I talked to a couple players on the way home, and they kind of understood. They were good with that.

As much as Darryl believed what he said, he appreciated what I said. We went back to the rink the next day knowing we couldn't do dumb things. That part was crucial, and I thought someone needed to say that. And I know the other assistants were sometimes a little intimidated by Darryl. But it needed to be said, and it was.

171

If you met Darryl, you might conclude that there would be no way our relationship would work well. He did get mad at me too many times when I played for him.

But Darryl is great at reading people, and even though I frustrated him at times, he knew my value. He knew we had similarities in how we looked at the game. He respected me as a player. And I think he knew I could relate to the players and serve as a counterweight to his approach.

Truthfully, I loved Darryl's approach to coaching. I can't stand coaches who suck up to players. If I didn't give Darryl my best effort, I knew I would hear about it. That's the way it should be.

The guys appreciated it, and we went back and swept both home games to win the series in four! We played the Coyotes in the conference final. They won the Pacific Division and had beaten Chicago in six games, then Nashville in five. Their goalie, Mike Smith, was playing really well, and their team was playing really well. It didn't matter.

We went in there and dominated them from start to finish. We played big, strong, and physical, and just manhandled them in their barn. We won Game 1, and Quickie shut 'em out in Game 2. We won Game 3, but lost Game 4 at home. We went back into their place and won Game 5 in overtime. The big kid, Dustin Penner, scored late in the OT. All year he was in and out of the lineup because he was out of shape. Darryl struggled with him. But Dustin had such a good postseason. He played with Mike Richards and Jeff Carter, and they played big. We were Western Conference champs for only the second time in franchise history and we had a chance to win the franchise's first Stanley Cup.

We went to New Jersey, which was cool for me since I played in New Jersey. Martin Brodeur was still there, and Larry Robinson was an assistant coach. Anže Kopitar scored in overtime of Game 1 and Carter scored the next game in overtime—both 2–1 finals—and we won the third game at home to go up 3–0. We won the first three games of every series. And now we could almost taste the Cup! We couldn't wait for Game 4. I had family down and everything. The game was in L.A., but it didn't work out. We lost Game 4, went back to New Jersey, and lost that one, too!

But coming back for Game 6, the guys were ready. Justin Williams won a Cup with Carolina; he'd been there before and he was clutch. He pulled the guys together for a players-only meeting. He talked to them before the game. There really wasn't much to say now. There wasn't much Darryl could say at that time. It was right in front of us. Game 6. Our building. Win the Cup.

The guys came out and were in such good control. They were wired, but it was all channeled in the right direction. From the word go they just played so well. We could have played all night and Jonathan Quick wasn't going to allow Jersey to beat us.

The game was scoreless midway through the first period when New Jersey's Steve Bernier boarded Rob Scuderi and was assessed a five-minute major. We scored three goals on it in a span of 3 minutes, 58 seconds.

Like I said, we might not score every time, but when we needed power play goals, we scored them. And that sequence broke it open, and we won the Stanley Cup.

The excitement of the crowd and the look of excitement on the guys' faces was unbelievable. The feeling was unbelievable. I had tears in my eyes. I had my daughter McKenna there and she came on the ice for the celebration afterward with me. I had one of the best people in the world, my daughter—and she was a hockey fan—with me. She loved it. I've got pictures of her and holding the Cup that I'll treasure for the rest of my life.

When my twins were young, their mother would joke that "Dad lived in the TV" because I traveled so much.

McKenna said during the book process that she "legitimately" believed I lived in the TV. When she was young, she would go to every game and could go in and out of the dressing room. She said she just assumed that everyone's dad played in the NHL.

173

"That was just our life," she said.

Only when she grew older did she catch on that her dad might have been "cooler" than she realized.

"Meeting people, their reaction was always, 'Oh my gosh, your dad is a legend!'" McKenna said. "'He's a really good hockey player.' Then I started to realize he wasn't just a hockey player; he was pretty badass!"

Now I was a badass celebrating a Stanley Cup title with my daughter at my side. It was a night to remember.

Los Angeles was my town. I grew up there as a player. To be able to come back and be a part of the franchise's first championship in over 40 years was really special.

We had the Cup in the locker room, too, for a long time. Just the Cup and the guys. The celebration went on for two or three days. I had my daughter with me for the parade. The boys had to be at the rink early—at 8:00 for pictures with the Cup—then went to the parade and back to Staples Center with everyone inside. I'll never forget it.

As a former NHLer, I understand that players win the Stanley Cup. But I felt like I helped some of them get to where they wanted to be. I was a positive person at a time when an upbeat, positive attitude was needed. I think it is easier for a skilled player who has been there to talk to skilled guys who are struggling to get there.

It was easier for some of the guys to come to me to discuss issues than it was to go to the head coach or an assistant. I was just a consultant. They could talk to me freely. Maybe I was just a good sounding board.

The Los Angeles players had the skill and Darryl knew how to point them in the right direction. But sometimes you just need a different perspective now and then to get everyone thinking about how to be better. Darryl knew I was a players' guy and he was fine with that because he understood they needed another ally. I know that night I was so proud of what those guys accomplished.

Goaltender Jonathan Quick said on live television and radio, "I just love these fucking guys." The place went crazy. It was awesome.

I was given my day with the Cup. Once in Canada, it was driven up to West Guilford. We had about 60 people at our home when it arrived.

One of the grand traditions of winning the Stanley Cup is the captain gets to choose who he will hand the Cup to first after he parades around the ice. It's quite an honor when the captain chooses you. Usually, the captain picks an older player who has been with the team a long time or a veteran who is winning his first cup. Everyone is always excited to see who the captain's choice will be.

I certainly thought about that when the Cup arrived and I immediately carried it over to my father, George Nicholls. Nobody had a greater influence on my career than he did. No one inspired me like he did.

My dad was the strong, silent type. Never showed much emotion. You could tell he was excited. He had such a shit-ass grin on his face. It was a cool time that he and I shared.

I had many memorable moments that day. My dad had built a canoe for me and my brothers years before and I took the Stanley Cup out on the lake in that canoe.

The Cup's handler was nervous about that plan. But I didn't take it very far into the lake. Just far enough to take a quality photograph. My dad had owned a hunting camp since 1961 and we took the Stanley Cup out there for photos. We advertised in advance that we were bringing the Stanley Cup to an arena in Haliburton. Everybody showed up with their kids.

On that day, I went up into my tree stand, dressed in camouflage apparel, bow and arrow beside me, and posed for a picture with a Stanley Cup. As far as I know, the only other person to shoot a photo in a tree stand was Pittsburgh Penguins coach Dan Bylsma.

My photo went viral. We heard from a guy from Wales who saw the photo and was curious about it.

When the handler took a nap, McKenna wanted to see if she could drink from the Cup. Turns out she can. We have the photos to prove it. That day couldn't have been any better.

CHAPTER 16

NOT THE SAME

WINNING THE 2012 STANLEY CUP was a wondrously wild ride. I loved every minute of that Los Angeles Kings magical playoff run. But I was just a passenger.

As much as I cherish my participation as a Kings consultant or Darryl Sutter's power play guy, or whatever you want to call me, I know the joy didn't come close to matching the emotion I would have felt had I won as a player.

Don't get me wrong: I celebrated that Kings championship. It was the first one in franchise history. I felt like I was part of it, and I was overjoyed to get my time with the Stanley Cup. I was humbled to receive a Stanley Cup championship ring.

I don't think for a minute that I played a big role in that championship, but I appreciated that multiple players told me afterward that they believed I had helped them find their confidence. They thought my role was significant.

It was gratifying that Darryl thought I had a role in getting everyone to look at the power play differently. I told Darryl that I appreciated that he gave me the opportunity to help, especially when his general manager seemed lukewarm on the idea.

But what I wanted most from my career was to win the Stanley Cup as a player and I didn't accomplish that. This didn't make up for that disappointment.

Not even close.

If I were to talk about this to someone for the first time, I wouldn't say I won the Stanley Cup. I would say, "I was part of a Stanley Cup run in a coaching role."

One disappointment about the Stanley Cup celebration was that I learned that my name wasn't engraved on it. I got everything you get when you win a Cup except the honor that you would covet the most: seeing your name on the Cup.

I thought that was going to happen. It hurt me, angered me a bit, not to be acknowledged in that way. A couple of players noticed my name wasn't there, noting that there were people there who didn't contribute to the on-ice success.

Although I can't be sure why my name didn't make the cut, I have been told that the general manager makes the final decision. That wasn't the first time a Dean Lombardi decision was unfavorable to me and a few months later I would discover it wouldn't be the last.

CHAPTER 17

BAD ENDING
TO GOOD CAREER

A LOCKOUT DELAYED THE 2012–13 NHL SEASON and gave me the opportunity to go home and hunt with my dad in the fall and early winter.

But when I was finished chasing after moose and deer, I ended up being in Dean Lombardi's sights again. In San Jose, he made the decision that ended my playing career. In Los Angeles, he made the decision that ended my coaching career.

The NHL and Players' Association finally agreed to a new collective bargaining agreement in time to start a 48-game season in January.

We were still all excited in L.A. over our Stanley Cup success in the spring. Darryl wanted me back. I was thrilled to be back.

Early in the season, the Kings were trailing 2–1 late against Vancouver at home, then came back with a goal in the final minute to force OT and won 3–2 in the shootout. We were all fired up afterward. I came running out of the dressing room and a woman working for the Kings who does a lot of stuff for me—just a friend of mine and a friend of my daughter's—was there, too.

She was walking by, and I was coming out at the same time where the hallway sort of forms a "T." I went to slap her on the hip to get her attention to say hello, and I caught more butt than hip. No reaction, just a laugh, and we kept going our separate ways.

The problem was a security guy saw the exchange and filed a report. We had a new security guard there every day. We all had badges to wear, and I hardly ever wore my badge. I don't know if he was pissed at me because I didn't wear my badge? Whatever. He filed it.

Shortly after I received a call from an AEG (Anschutz Entertainment Group) representative and was told to come in for a meeting.

I was informed what I did was wrong, and I was being suspended. I absolutely lost my mind. I explained my action was an accident. They wanted to meet a couple of days later, but I couldn't be around the players or the team in the meantime. I received another call with a message that the meeting had been moved. So, I returned the call and left the woman in human resources a voicemail. And it was a memorable one. I was swearing like a sailor.

"This is a fucking joke, it's bullshit," I said. "Where I hit (her) was an accident. I meant to do this, I did that."

I was swearing at my situation, not the woman on the phone. But that didn't seem to matter to anyone. I received another call, this time from a guy with AEG downtown asking what I said to the woman? Did I swear?

And I said, "Yeah, I did. I was pissed. I did something, and I was explaining it."

Meanwhile, someone high in the Kings organization came to me and said, "Look, this happened to me. I did community service and that was it."

I thought I would be fine.

On the day of the final meeting, I first met Dean Lombardi and team president Luc Robitaille.

"Look, you've got to get on your knees and apologize," Dean said.

"Dean, I didn't do anything wrong," I replied. "I made a mistake. This isn't what I meant to do. She's my friend. Ask her."

I'd met with this person privately many times, and I was sure she would corroborate with the fact that I never once acted inappropriately.

I meant to hit her hip and missed. It wasn't that I grabbed her. So be it. I made a mistake.

"Do this, and we'll get through it," Dean said.

The three of us headed downtown to the meeting. We waited outside the room to meet with AEG representatives at 10:00, and I could hear laughter behind the closed door. We went in—I had Dean to my right and Luc to my left—and we were facing two ladies from human resources with AEG.

One of them handed me a letter.

"We're terminating your contract right now," she said.

"What are you talking about?" I asked.

She said I had to go to anger management. So, I'm not getting fired for sexual harassment, but I have to go to anger management? I can always use that; I'm the first to admit I have an anger issue. And I did swear, but I didn't verbally abuse the lady because not once did I attack her. I was explaining the situation and, yes, I was swearing. As it was explained to me, the plan was to go to anger management, work through my problem, and then, when I was done, Dean would be allowed to rehire me.

I looked at them and said, "Dean's not hiring me back. He's not doing anything now."

Right then he could have stepped up and helped me, but he didn't. He could have asked to put me on probation under his supervision. He could have had my back.

"What are you talking about?" he asked.

I said, "You haven't done anything for me. You could tell them, 'Hey, I'll look after him and if he gets out of line...' but you didn't do that for me, you did nothing for me."

He threw me under the bus and let them fire me.

But I hoped I was wrong. I attended anger management classes, working with someone from AEG for 2–3 weeks. I had seven or eight sessions. It all went well. The AEG people told me I was good to go. I should have known I was excited for no good reason. I went back and there was no chance in hell Dean would hire me back. Once again, I was fucked by Dean for reasons that I didn't understand.

Darryl was sympathetic, but powerless in this situation.

"Look, there's nothing I can do," Darryl said. "AEG and Dean have to let this go. They have to bring you back. This is their decision."

Dean wouldn't budge. And that's how my hockey life ended. He wouldn't stand up for me. I don't know why Dean decided he didn't like me. Darryl is a good judge of character, fair and principled, and he always wanted me around. When Dean recruited me to San Jose, he seemed sold on my strengths. But something changed his mind and I'm not sure what it was. I did what he asked me to do in San Jose.

What bothered me was that they wouldn't let me talk to anyone in the organization, the players, or the media. They kept the month-long process hush-hush. But people knew I wasn't with the team. Rumors were out there that it was about sexual harassment.

But I didn't sexually harass anyone. I just missed my attempt to get someone's attention. What eventually cost me was anger and swearing in reaction to the situation.

All I know was this was the third time that Lombardi had a chance to do something nice for me and chose not to do it.

CHAPTER 18

BIG HITS AND
TABOO GOLF

HALL OF FAME WINGER LUC ROBITAILLE tells a good story of how I welcomed him to his first Los Angeles Kings training camp by pancaking him with a hit at center ice.

"We were doing a drill," Robitaille said. "I came across the ice like I would in junior and Bernie drilled me so hard it knocked my helmet off."

Robitaille said it was an eye-opening experience about what it was like to play in the NHL. Even your teammates will deck you if you aren't paying attention. I always felt it's part of your job to help prepare your teammates for NHL competition. But that hit was the start of a good friendship.

"Bernie was a skill guy but even he drilled me," Robitaille said. "I remember thinking, *Wow, this is the NHL; there's a difference.* I got cut and sent back to junior."

But the wake-up hit is just part of our story. I knew Robitaille had top level offensive ability and when he showed up the following season, I told him, "Kid, I'm going to play with you."

Robitaille recalls scoring a couple of goals and then trying to fight someone above his weight class.

"This was a real tough guy," Robitaille recalled in telling the story for this book. "He beat the crap out of me and when I was down on the ice and cut, the one guy I heard jump on the pile was Bernie. He jumped in to save me. I recall him telling the other guy, 'Stop it, you're going to kill him.' I knew right then and there Bernie was going to take care of me."

Robitaille's story tells what it meant to me to be someone's teammate better than I can explain it. I'm proud of the fact that throughout my career I was known as a good teammate. My dad taught me at an early age that you need to look out for your teammates like they are family. You protect them, lift their spirits, do whatever you can to help them find success.

Late in the 1987–88 season, the season before Wayne Gretzky arrived, Luc and I were not playing together. He had 48 goals with two road games left in Calgary and Edmonton.

I went to coach Robbie Ftorek with a request.

"Let me play with the kid, and I'll get him his 50th," I said.

At the morning skate, I told him, "Lucky, get open tonight, and I'm going to get your 50th."

Luc recalls that he had "seven or eight chances" that night and he scored twice to reach 50. In the next game against the Oilers, I set him up often enough to score three goals.

To the best of Luc's recollection, that was the only two games we played together. "I'll never forget [those games]," Luc said.

My relationships with my teammates were one of the most memorable aspects of being an NHL player. You strive to play in the NHL because you want to play, compete, and measure your skill against the world's top players. But when you arrive in the NHL, you realize that the joy and some of your fondest memories come from sharing the journey with a dressing room full of athletes who have your back.

And everyone knew I had their back. Even though I wasn't really a fighter, my teammates knew I would be there for them if there was trouble on the ice. Luc. Wayne Gretzky. Joe Murphy. Tie Domi. Gary Suter. Chris Chelios. Owen Nolan. Tony Granato. I could go on for a long time. It's probably similar to being in the military. You end up with a list of lasting friendships. You don't see each other after you go your separate way, but when you do get together you pick up where you left off. You have shared memories and a bond that survives the time away from each other.

I tried to rescue my teammates even if they didn't want to be rescued, like the time Granato was battling with Florida's Ed Jovanovski.

Granato was more than a little surprised when I came at Jovo like I was leading the charge in the movie *Braveheart*. You know I was charged up because I was suspended for the cross-check I planted on Jovanovski.

"Bernie, what are you doing?" he asked. "I've done this a million times. I can handle myself. Even if I'm going to get beat up, it's okay."

But it wasn't okay with me. I'm not going to accept an opponent pounding on a teammate.

"Ton," I said. "I'm never going to let that happen to you."

Not on my watch. Never going to happen. That is not how my dad raised me as a player.

"That's the brotherhood and being part of a locker room," Tony said when we discussed the incident for this book.

That's how I see it.

I signed with the Sharks a week before Tony did and I had called and made a pitch for him to come to San Jose. He called me a "good recruiter."

Everyone knew I liked to have a good time when I played, but not everyone knew that I could stir up trouble. Marty McSorley did.

"When I got traded to L.A. I remember right away thinking, *Okay, I'm going to have to keep my eyes open,*" McSorley said. "There were going to be times I was going to have to stick up for Bernie because people were going to want to kick his butt."

As McSorley put it, I was one of those players who "would throw a shoulder into a guy's chin when he didn't expect it."

He said opponents couldn't be sure if I was going "to steal the puck from you or run you into the boards."

As much as coaches liked the fact that I stood up for teammates and liked to hit, they didn't much like that when players hung with me there was a chance they might violate a curfew or break a team rule or two.

My buddy Gary Leeman was an opponent, playing for the Toronto Maple Leafs, when I led him astray.

The Maple Leafs had beat the Vancouver Canucks one night and then flew to Los Angeles early in the morning for another game that night. Back-to-back games. Gary should have gone to the LAX Marriott to get some rest. But I persuaded him to golf with me.

Of course, Gary didn't say a word to anyone on his team about our plans. He gave his bag to his roommate to place in their room.

"I'll see you at the game," he told Luke Richardson.

He didn't bring his golf clubs. He wasn't dressed for golf. He just looked like a guy going to meet a friend for lunch. But his hope for secrecy was blown up when I drove up to the Marriott in a convertible, dressed in golf attire. I parked right behind the shuttle that transported the players from the airport.

"And he's got this big tour golf bag sitting in the other seat, as if [the scene] wasn't blatant enough," Gary said in the telling of the story. "Anyone watching knew where we were going."

Back then, players looked forward to the road trip to Los Angeles just for the warmth. It was the only warm weather city. This was a treat for Gary, although there was some risk involved. Kings players did golf on game days, but the Maple Leafs organization considered it taboo. Violation for the offense was a lecture, fine, or both.

We played almost a full round of golf, enjoyed some lunch, and then headed for the Forum. Gary got into the dressing room before his teammates. Some of the guys looked at him suspiciously when they entered the room. But everything seemed normal, and he thought he had gotten away with an ill-advised round of golf.

It wasn't until the warmups that Gary realized he had not rubbed sunscreen into his face before we golfed. The usually pale Gary had a face as red as a tomato.

"Basically, both teams were staring at me," Gary remembered.

As the years slip away, you forget scores and names. But you recall entertaining days like Gary and I had. When we see each other, we always have a chuckle over that day on the course.

When I was in San Jose, I also managed to lead Patrick Marleau into some minor trouble when he was an 18-year-old rookie in 1997–98.

Sutter had declared the morning skate optional, and I convinced Marleau to come with me for a massage and a pre-game meal. I told him he needed to relax.

It was an unwritten rule that optional skates are never optional for rookies. I knew that was the case, but I didn't think Sutter would hold Marleau to that. He ended up being a 32-point scorer as a rookie. He adapted to the league quickly and you could tell he was going to be an impact player.

Lombardi had wanted me to mentor Marleau and we became tight. He trusted my judgment and I felt like he needed a break from practice.

But it turned out I was wrong in my assessment of how Sutter would react to that situation. He scratched Marleau from the game that night. Of course, I played. Marleau was mad at Darryl, not me. But I felt guilty because he followed my advice to take time off.

On April 19, 2021, Marleau played his 1,768th NHL game to break Gordie Howe's all-time record for games played. That is an amazing feat. Gordie is a legend, iconic as it gets. The Sharks put together a tribute video and my brief message included my congratulations and a reminder that I cost him a game 24 years before.

I told him I was a little bit worried that he was going to end up one game short of Mr. Hockey's record. If that had happened, I would have felt pretty bad.

I always played with intensity, but I couldn't wear a game face 24 hours per day. If you talk to anyone who played with me in Chicago, they will talk about my escapades as if I was a star of sitcom, not a hockey player.

It's been 26 years since I played in Chicago, but teammates remember some of the antics that Joe Murphy and I were involved in like they occurred yesterday. We were always fighting to be on time for the morning stretches on game day and some practices.

"We were getting ready to practice after getting beat the night before when Darryl came in and just gave it to us," former Chicago defenseman Gary Suter recalled. "We noticed Bernie and Joe weren't there yet. They used to stroll in right before practice. Coach said we were going to have a bag practice and stormed out of the room. Right after he left, Bernie and Joe walked in late. Wearing his fur coat, sunglasses, and drinking a milkshake, Bernie said, 'What's up, fellas?'"

"The room just burst out laughing. That was so Bernie. Of course, he had to go in and explain why he and Murph were late."

Talking about Murphy and me, Suter added, "It was always comic relief when those two clowns were around."

Sometimes I didn't have to work hard to find a partner to have some fun. McSorley remembers the time he and I pranked Glen Sather. McSorley and I were playing with San Jose at the time.

"This was after we both played in Edmonton and knew how much Glen liked the suits he wore and how he always kept his car clean," McSorley said. "When our bus pulled up, we saw Glen's car outside the ramp in Edmonton. [We] came out after the morning skate with a couple of cans of shaving cream and just plastered Slats' car."

Of course, Glen uncovered who the culprits were and when we came into our locker room after the game, Marty and I found that the pockets of our suit coats were filled with shaving cream.

Not all my buddies were corrupted by my efforts to enjoy life. Tony Granato could resist the urge to go as far as I would go in the name of having a good time.

One time, I asked Tony to hang out with me because Michael Jordan was in town.

Tony grew up in Downers Grove, Illinois, and I could tell that he was thinking, *Wow, my one chance to spend an evening with MJ?*

But the Sharks had a 10:00 PM curfew that night in anticipation of an afternoon game the next day.

"I just can't do it," Tony said.

Jordan and I were out late hitting the clubs. The next day, I was in the dressing room pulling on my gear. I looked over at Tony and gave him a wink. I let him know he had missed a good time.

CHAPTER 19

FOR MURPH, PROBIE, TODD, AND GARY

WHEN I WAS PLAYING for the New York Rangers, I witnessed Tie Domi and Bob Probert locked in a hockey fight that had the intensity of a WBC heavyweight championship bout.

Replays showed about 100 punches were thrown in the battle. As I recall, Probie threw about 60 and Tie fired 40.

The next day, Tie's head was so battered and bruised he couldn't comfortably wear his helmet.

When I was with San Jose, I saw my teammate Todd Ewen fight another teammate, Tim Hunter, in training camp in preparation for the season. I guess tough guys need practice, too. But how much did Ewen and Probert hurt their long-term health by playing the way they did?

Probert was my roommate in Chicago in 1995–96. He turned 31 right after the season, and 14 years later he was dead. The official cause was heart failure, but an autopsy of his brain showed he suffered from the degenerative brain disease chronic traumatic encephalopathy (CTE) at the time of his death.

Ewen fatally shot himself at age 49. The first autopsy of his brain came back negative for CTE, but subsequent exams by Boston University CTE experts showed lesions consistent with stage 2 CTE. What role did hockey-related concussions and CTE play in his suicide?

Even though most former NHL players would presumably do it all again, there are questions being raised about the risks of playing the sport. For example, can we do a better job of preventing and treating concussions? And who is responsible for taking care of players who need costly medical care later in their lives?

These questions were at the heart of why I decided to become a spokesman for a series of concussion-related lawsuits filed by retired players against the NHL starting in 2013.

Retired players challenged the league for having minimized concussion risks for decades. In our opinion, the league profited off violence while ignoring warnings from the scientific community. Players were not educated to the substantially higher risk of developing brain-related diseases such as Alzheimer's and dementia, not to mention depression and anxiety.

When I signed on for this cause, I felt like I was standing up for Probie, Todd, and many others.

Gary Leeman, one of my best friends in the game, once scored 51 goals in a season. But today, almost 25 years after his career is over, he struggles with medical issues. He suffers from frequent headaches and vision problems. He believes he has developed a short temper connected to the numerous concussions he suffered. Gary can't be sure how many concussions he endured because concussions went undiagnosed or unreported when we played. In those days, we didn't have a concussion protocol.

But Gary is sure that a deflected slap shot by Al MacInnis that struck him in the back of head was one of the injuries causing some of his symptoms. MacInnis was viewed as having the NHL's hardest shot when he played. Gary was an outspoken victim during the lawsuit.

Not all that long ago Joe Murphy and I were having too much fun together playing for the Chicago Blackhawks, Edmonton Oilers, and San Jose Sharks. Today, as this book is being written, Murphy is homeless. It's hard to know where he is from week to week. He is lost within his own mind.

He was also one of my best friends. And Murph suffered a terrible concussion that changed him completely. He fractured his skull on a hit into the boards in 1991, but he came back and played in the same game. That's how different the NHL was back when I played. Murph was a No. 1 overall pick in the 1986 NHL draft, and now he's not the same player or even the same person. His daughter, Krystal, described him as being competitive, funny, smart, and someone who wanted to make those around him laugh. But, as the years went on during his NHL career, his personality changed dramatically. Joe became moody, quick-tempered, and agitated. He didn't seem to enjoy the game as much and he wasn't the same happy-go-lucky guy we all knew.

After his career Joe displayed a lot of symptoms associated with brain trauma. He had depression and memory loss, which turned into substance abuse. We feared he could act on suicidal thoughts. Murph became estranged from his family and ended up homeless in a remote part of Ontario.

It hurts when you see friends become screwed up and you know it's probably from all the concussions they suffered. It was just a game we were playing. When the opportunity to speak up and be part of the lawsuit was brought to me, I thought it was such an easy decision. I was told I was going to stand up for the players. That's what I always did when I was playing in the NHL.

I wasn't receiving any money for this, but we were trying to get money for former players who needed it. I was all in. This was never about me. This was my chance to stand up for guys I cared about. It was always a brotherhood for me. The NHL culture is to battle for the guy beside you. I've had more people that I can think of take punches in the head for me. I had a ton of guys who stuck up for me, went to war for me. I played with guys who died at a very young age.

And I consider everyone in the NHL a brother to me, whether I played with them or not. That's the great thing about our league: guys stick together.

I do have my own post-career medical issues. I get dizzy often. And my memory is poor about certain facts I should know. There isn't a day that goes by that I don't get dizzy when I put my head down on the pillow.

Amazingly, I was never diagnosed with a concussion when I played in the NHL. I broke my jaw when I got elbowed—I think I might have received a concussion on that. And I got hit 10 minutes later, too, because I didn't rest after the first one.

I received 25 stitches over my eye because I got hit with a hockey stick another time. If you get split open for 25 stitches, I'm pretty sure it comes with a concussion. I hit Valeri Kamensky at the blue line in Chicago. I lacerated my spleen; our heads collided. I was dizzy and could hardly make my way back to the bench. I was never diagnosed with a concussion on that one either.

I kept playing, never missing a shift. One night in San Jose, Gary Roberts kicked my feet out from under me. My head hit the ice. That was the worst I ever felt for a head injury.

I sat on the bench for a little bit waiting to get cleared and then went out and played again.

When I was being deposed for the lawsuit, I explained all of this. But the lawyer doing the deposition could not grasp where I've had a problem.

Another night in San Jose I was eating a potato chip and chipped a tooth. I went to the dentist, and he discovered all my teeth had been fractured from being punched and elbowed in the face. My front four teeth are not really mine. But I've never had a concussion?

That's what they were trying to tell me. It was so disappointing because the NHL officials know how rough this game has been for decades. Look at what they have in place now: the protocol and spotters sitting in the press box to identify players showing signs of a concussion.

We have those safeguards in place today, and league officials are trying to say we didn't have any problems in the 1960s, '70s, and '80s. Do they believe that hockey became dangerous overnight? Do they believe it became dangerous the day before the concussion protocol began?

My opinion is that today's safeguards are an admission that more should have been done in my era. In today's game, we hear people saying there is less hitting than there used to be in the game. "We need to get hitting back in the game," people say.

To me, that's more evidence that we had a problem that wasn't addressed. If we are trying to protect players today, then we should have been doing it years ago because the game was rougher than it is today.

League officials knew they screwed up when they didn't address the concussion issue before.

The NHL could have been the league that cares. Commissioner Gary Bettman or another league official could have said, "You know what? We're going to take care of the guys who need it. That may be five players, or 10 players, it might be more than 100. It doesn't matter. We will take care of them."

But you know that's not what the NHL is going to do. The NHL is going to protect ownership's money.

What I wanted was a plan where money went to the players who needed it. That's the way it was supposed to be. Instead, both sides decided to settle late in 2018 for $18.9 million. The distribution plan: everyone receiving $22,000.

My reaction: No fucking way.

The settlement was ridiculous and didn't come close to addressing the problem. In addition to the cash payment, the players received up to $75,000 in medical treatments for players who test positive in two or more tests and a "Common Good Fund" of $2.5 million for retired players in need.

The players who really needed help didn't get enough.

By contrast, the NFL settlement, according to the *Associated Press*, will require the NFL to pay out $1.5 billion over 65 years.

A total of 318 NHL players signed up to receive money. We had people who signed up that played only maybe five games in the NHL.

Down the line, if guys have problems, this wouldn't take care of all of them. A one-time payment now wasn't the answer.

The settlement was reached a few months after a federal judge denied class-action status for the retired players. Had U.S. District Judge Susan Richard Nelson granted the class-action request, there would have been one group of all living former NHL players and another group of retired players diagnosed with neurological diseases or conditions. Had we been granted class-action, more than 5,000 former players could have joined the lawsuit.

This lawsuit could have been handled better. We never had high-profile players, such as Wayne Gretzky or Mario Lemieux, to take a stand.

Some former players, particularly the ones working for NHL teams as scouts or broadcasters or ambassadors, etc., were afraid to join the lawsuit because they might lose jobs or their connection to their team.

One former player told me that he was told if he wanted his son to play in the NHL, he shouldn't attach his name to the lawsuit. I had a couple of players working for a Canada-based NHL team who bailed on the lawsuit because their bosses told them it wouldn't be in their best interest to be involved in the lawsuit.

I've had many people involved in the lawsuit tell me they feel like they have been blackballed because of their participation. I can say it happened to me.

I had a buddy who wanted to run a business opportunity through the NHL. He thought he could help them make some money. I told him I'd call the league and try to make an appointment for him. I called and asked for Deputy Commissioner Bill Daly's office and reached his secretary.

"It's Bernie Nicholls and I want to set up an appointment with Mr. Daly about a product that might help them make some money," I said.

She took my number. Not hearing back, I called again. I reminded the secretary who I was and that I had called before looking to make an appointment with Mr. Daly.

She paused for a second.

"Oh yeah, I talked to Mr. Daly, and they're not interested at this time in what you have," she said.

And I said, "Ma'am, I never told you what I have. I never told you what it was about."

The simple truth was they wanted nothing to do with me, regardless of what I was bringing to the table.

Despite my 18 years in the NHL, and all that I went through, Daly wouldn't give me the time of day now. And all I did was stand up for my brothers.

That's the sad part that came out of this lawsuit. As teammates, we lost players who took their lives. And none of this is their fault. And that's too bad. It bothered me when these guys were settling. I'd put my neck out on the line for players who needed it, not to win $22,000 for anyone who put their name on a list. That bothered me, too. I was a loser on both ends.

The settlement wasn't nearly enough, and the league seems to have blackballed me.

Obviously, the lawyers will end up making more money than the players who need it. If you played in the NHL, you should have insurance for life. Period. Some players are having a tough time with a variety of medical issues. I did an event with Corey Hirsch, who played in goal for Vancouver and three other teams in the league for seven seasons. He's gone through depression.

Corey told me a story of how he took his mom to the Empire State Building when he was playing for the Rangers. This was when I was playing in New Jersey. He told his mother, "If I could, I would jump."

Scary incidents are happening with former players. Another sad layer of the Hirsch story is his girlfriend at the time did commit suicide.

Former players need help out there, and the NHL turned its back because it doesn't want to get stuck for the tab. But if the NHL won't look after the players, who will?

After the settlement, former players reached out for me and thanked me for at least trying to hold the league accountable. I think anyone who looked seriously at the situation would do what I did. As disappointed as I was in the result, I respect everyone who stood up against the league. I hope they respect me. I'd do it again.

And if the NHL never acknowledges me or does another thing for me, I'm still going to love the NHL, just like I love every team I ever played for. The NHL may be flawed, but I loved every minute I played in that league.

CHAPTER 20

JUST A SMALL-TOWN BOY

WHEN I WAS YOUNG, my parents might have thought I had a better chance of being a juvenile delinquent than an NHL star.

I was a bad kid. Oh my God, I was terrible.

We had one store in town, the West Guilford Store, and I stole from it multiple times. I'd go in there with a lunch pail and fill it up. Candy. Potato chips. Other food items. Hockey tape. Bait. I had variety in my pilfering. It was like picking items off a buffet.

Once, I went into the store with my next-door cousin Wade. A little older than me, Wade wore a Ski-Doo suit. It was bulky and offered plenty of pockets, providing more opportunities to stuff candy and other food items without being conspicuous.

The guy running the store was usually alone. He'd be in the back and often didn't know we had entered the place. We'd fill our clothes with stolen goods and be gone before he returned to the counter. More often than not, it was the perfect $5 to $7 heist.

Another time I stole bait and was walking home just as my dad was coming out. Panicked by his presence, I hooked my ill-gotten bait on the back of our car. It didn't occur to me that he was coming out to drive somewhere. My dad drove off with the bait clanking against the back of the car.

When my dad caught me with my ill-gotten hockey tape, he marched me back to the store and forced me to confess my crime.

I did get caught sticking bubble gum up my sleeve by a lady at the store one time. Another time I was with my best friend, Dwight Sisson, and he stuffed *Playboy* magazines under his shirt and down his pants. We were walking out and the lady—Marge Bain, I'll never forget her name—stopped us. She poked Dwight in the stomach and asked, "What's this?"

My troublemaking was not limited to petty theft. After I was nabbed stealing the gum, I set a field on fire next to the store. I don't know what I was thinking—trying to burn the place down, I guess that's what I was doing? But you really don't think it through when you are a kid. When I arrived home after my fire-starting, Mum was on the phone. They called her from the store because they knew it was me.

If there was any trouble, all my mum would have to say to me was, "Wait until your father comes home."

I knew what that meant. It wasn't good for me.

My mum and dad—Marjorie and George Nicholls—had five children. My oldest sister, Alberta, is three years older than me. I was next, then Cheryl (13 months younger), David (three years younger) and, finally, Erin (nine years younger). So, in order, our names start with A, B, C, D, and E! Erin, who like Cheryl still lives in West Guilford, boasts red hair so everyone calls him "Red."

Dad did the disciplining. With Mum, you were good. I tell people to this day: my dad beat the shit out of me. Not literally, but with spankings. It was always a spanking, never a punch. One time he might have used a piece of wood to paddle me on the butt. I don't know why, but I just kept doing horrible things.

I remember my mum telling me when I was a kid, "You know, it hurts your dad more than it hurts you, right?"

"Yeah, okay, I don't think so, Mum," I would say.

It's something you don't understand until you have kids. Once I became a parent, I realized how challenging it is to be a parent. I recall one time I just grabbed my son, Flynn. To this day, that memory scares me when I think about it.

When I look back and think about what I put my dad through, I think, *Oh, my God!*

There's nothing worse. I was a real bad kid. I have no problem with spankings on the butt. Every bad kid deserves that, some more than others, and I got everything I deserved.

When we asked my younger sister, Cheryl Cooper, about my adolescent years she pointed out correctly that I wasn't "big into school."

"He couldn't sit still long enough. I know one of the teachers assigned Bernie a hockey-related project just to keep him interested," Cheryl said. "He was a typical boy. He'd get into trouble, and he'd get me into trouble because I'd always follow him around."

My dad drove a truck for a living, usually on local runs. Sometimes he'd go away for a week at a time and have to stay on a job. But it didn't happen very often.

West Guilford was such a small town that employment options were limited. You're either a logger, a truck driver, or a skilled laborer such as an electrician or plumber. My mum's brother drove a log truck until the day he died. Another brother drove trucks, and the other milled at the lumberyard.

For Mum to manage the house with five kids was plenty of work when I look back on it now. Dinner was always on the table for my dad when he got home at night. Mum and Dad were at opposite ends of the table. I was next to the right of Dad. Alberta was on his left with Cheryl and David next. That was before Red came along. And Dad never said much at the kitchen table. There was no dinner conversation—at least not from Dad. He was there to eat.

My mum came from a large family, too. She was one of seven children. Three of her brothers and two sisters also lived in West Guilford.

One brother lived across the road from our house, and another in a small house maybe 50 yards away. I always had cousins to play with.

There was no street address at our home, just a dirt driveway and open space with bush and land behind that led to water. This was home for Mum, Dad, and my two sisters and brothers. The house had one bathroom, an unfinished basement where water came in, and maybe 1,300 square feet of living space for a family of seven. I wouldn't have traded it for the world.

It was not like it is for today's children. We never spent much time inside. There was nothing to do in the house. Everything I did was outside—tobogganing, ball hockey, ice hockey, trapping—we'd always be doing something. Obviously, there wasn't much traffic. And when we played hockey on the road—you see it in movies—we'd yell "car!" and move the nets. The main road was asphalt, and it was good to play on, but none of our driveways were paved, and they're still not to this day.

We owned hunting dogs on the land behind us. I could go through the bush out back all the way to the lake. It was maybe 300 yards, and we'd go back there trapping. I remember falling into the lake up to my waist one time when I was young in either January or February, and it was cold! I had jeans on that froze up and it was tough to even move! Kids running around on their own wasn't an issue in my hometown.

To drive from the West Guilford sign to the sign on the other side was not even a mile. Everything was right around there: all my friends and cousins, the school, the rink, and the store. They were all 200-to-400 yards away. There was a ballpark at the school where we'd play baseball, and there was even a nine-hole golf course on farmland. It was basically a cow pasture.

We were never home until late at night, too, because it didn't get dark until 9:00 in the summertime. What little we had in our tired town we had all to ourselves. If we did anything inside it was watching TV. Well, watching whatever Dad had on because he controlled the TV. It was so different then—and it was so good.

We had two channels on our television—3 and 11—and you had to sometimes adjust the antenna that was just outside my bedroom window to get reception. I had to open the window and turn and twist it to get the signal just right.

Mum or Dad would be in front of the TV in the family room shouting, "A little more...a little more." And then, "Whoa, whoa, whoa!"

Sometimes it was 40-below outside at home and I had to open the window, throw some water on the antenna to get it turned to watch the hockey game!

I started skating at the age of three. I was born pigeon-toed at birth, but that wasn't going to stop me. I had to slip my feet into boots and wear a metal brace to bed every night when I was young.

"Because of where we come from, there's really only two things to do: hockey in the winter and baseball in the summer," my sister Alberta Upton said. "And Bernie was awesome at both. And, as the oldest, I remember Bernie having to wear those braces on his legs—big metal things—and he would take them off as soon as he could. He skated and walked funny, but Bernie achieved a lot even though he had that bad foot."

Even when I was very young—maybe Grade 2 or 3—I was dominant in hockey. I would pick one other guy and a couple of girls and we'd take on everyone. The team I picked would beat everybody.

I felt so fortunate to grow up in West Guilford. I've always said country folks—and I consider myself one of those—had an advantage over city people when it came to hockey because of ice time. I'd hear stories of city kids having practices at 6:00 or 7:00 in the morning because that was the only available ice time. City rinks were in such demand. They couldn't get as much ice time as we would. We could skate and play any time, all the time, in our small town.

Dad made a rink in front of the house in the winter, and we'd play street hockey in the summer. There was a rink at the school, too, and it had a long string of 50-watt lights that kept the surface lit at night. When I was a little older, I'd just play there as long as I could every day.

My dad would have to come get me because I wouldn't go home on my own.

Besides the rink my dad made on the frozen front lawn, we lived next to a lake we could shovel off and skate there, too. So, there was never a shortage of ice for us. And hockey was such a big part of our family.

I played other sports, too. When I was older, and before I signed my first NHL contract, I went to the Summer Games for Ontario and won a silver medal for fast-pitch baseball. I played a lot of baseball. I usually played for two or three teams. One summer, I played for five.

I played high school football in Grade 9—just the one year—and was the quarterback before I left to go to Woodstock to play hockey. Why did I play quarterback? I guess that's a position for your best athletes, and I could throw the ball really well. I loved playing football.

I honestly loved every sport. I liked tennis. And I didn't start playing golf actually until I got to L.A. But, obviously, when I was young, hockey and baseball were huge, and then football. Hockey was No. 1, and I was lucky to have people around me to push me and recognize I had a chance to play for a long, long time.

One of those people was my dad, and another was my first cousin, Craig Stamp. He is the son of one of my mother's three brothers. Craig was seven years older than me, and he had helped my coach in Haliburton.

My dad knew I was serious about hockey. He also knew I needed to play with and against better players. And I needed to play somewhere I might get seen. That wasn't going to happen in Haliburton where I had played all my minor hockey. Scouts weren't flocking there.

Craig was a top-notch hockey player. He played major junior and had a tryout with the Toronto Maple Leafs. He ended up playing senior hockey in Woodstock, Ontario, a city of approximately 40,000 that was a four-hour drive from West Guilford and 142 kilometers, or 88 miles, west of Toronto.

"You know, you should let Bernie come down and play Junior B. I think it'd be really good for him," Craig said.

Craig was married, and they had settled in Woodstock. The idea was for me to live with them. The Junior B team was the Woodstock Navy Vets.

Woodstock was a long way from West Guilford. But Dad liked the plan. Mum really liked the idea that I would be staying with relatives. I was 16 when I moved to Woodstock.

Luckily for me, and I say this all the time about Canadian boys, one of the toughest tests we face is leaving home at a young age to pursue hockey. You need to see if you can realize your potential. And being away from home is part of that journey. That's what was tough for my brother, David. I was fortunate that I got to live with my cousin.

It was the right decision to go to Woodstock. Even though I was one of the younger players there, I was one of the better players. I was drafted in the eighth round of the 1978 Ontario Hockey League Draft by the Kingston Canadians.

I didn't make the team the first season, but I did the second season and then I spent 100 percent of my time concentrating on being the best hockey player I could be.

Well, maybe it wasn't quite 100 percent about hockey.

Kingston to West Guilford is a three-hour drive if the weather is good. You aren't going to commute. This time I had no relatives in town. My billet ended up being with Vern and Sylvia Walters. They owned a fur store and a drive-in movie theatre. I would work on weekends at the fur store where I bought a full-length fur coat. I'd wear that around everywhere, and it even made the trip to Los Angeles. That coat really started my interest in fashion and dressing sharply.

I came home to the Walters' home one night after a game and Sylvia was sitting by herself at the table with a bag of weed. I knew nothing about marijuana or other drugs. I still don't drink, don't smoke, and never did drugs. Sylvia owned a big radio and CD player that she wouldn't let us touch. And sitting next to it was a big bong. I had no idea what that was. That's the absolute truth. No clue what it was.

Her family could afford to only buy half a pound of marijuana, and I came up with an idea for the other half. We lived near these four-plex apartments across the street at St. Lawrence College in Kingston. And I knew some of the girls going to school there.

So, Sylvia would buy a half pound for $40 an ounce and I would buy the other half pound and sell it to the students for $60 an ounce. I made $160 profit on a $320 investment. And that was in 1980. I wonder what it would cost today?

CHAPTER 21

MY DAD, MY HERO

IN 2012, I WAS IN MY HOMETOWN, driving near where I usually hunt, when I spotted this big 10-point buck. I sped up my truck and headed home to get my bow. It was out of season. But I was determined to hunt that buck.

When my brothers and I were younger, we hunted and fished out of season.

This deer was fucking huge. But as I was grabbing my gear, my dad said, "I wish you wouldn't do that."

That's all he said. I can still picture him sitting in the chair saying those words. He didn't tell me not to do it. But he made it clear that he didn't think it was a good idea to hunt illegally.

"Okay," I said.

I didn't hunt that day.

At that point, I was 51 years old and had played 1,127 NHL games. I had been retired for 13 years. I wouldn't have listened to anyone else. But I always listened to my dad. That's how much respect I had for him. The older I got the more I realized how much he meant to me.

My dad taught me everything I know about hunting and hockey, and much of what I know about life.

The kitchen floor of my childhood home in West Guilford had battle scars from the many times George Nicholls taught his son how to play the game. The light beige linoleum was worn, scuffed, and gouged because that's where my dad helped me perfect my faceoff skill.

My mother didn't like our nightly ritual at all. It drove her nuts. She begged us to go "anywhere but here." We had carpet in the living room. That was out. We preferred her 10 × 10 foot kitchen. The floor was nice and smooth so you could snap the puck back. The lighting was good. The space was right: not too small, not so big that we would be chasing the puck all night.

My sister Alberta recalls that my sisters took turns dropping the puck.

"The black tape on the stick wasn't good for the floor," Alberta recalled. "That was just life. We never asked them to stop because we wanted to hear the TV. There were only two stations, and it was probably on hockey anyway."

Faceoffs kept happening as life went on in the kitchen.

"I'd be doing the dishes and trying to stay out of the way," my sister Cheryl remembered. "But I'd still get the stick in the old shins. It never slowed Bernie down. Dad had a mission; he was teaching him how to get better at it, and it didn't matter what we were trying to do in the kitchen."

These kitchen practice sessions are why I took so much pride in faceoffs during my 18-season NHL career. It didn't matter what the game situation was; I wanted to win the draw. It could be a 5–0 game with one second left. I was still going to win it. My dad taught me the importance of faceoffs.

My dad taught me several lessons in our kitchen, and not just about faceoffs.

When I was 10 years old, he told me, "If you want to play in the NHL, you can't be drinking."

He offered no other explanation, and I didn't ask for any. He knew I had been around drinking since I was young. My mom and dad drank. My dad liked rye and Mum would drink a beer. They would go to my uncle's house on a Saturday night, and everyone would be singing, playing poker, watching hockey, and having a good time. Maybe it was just my dad's way of saying, "Don't be drinking when you are 15."

But I took his words to heart, and I said, "Fuck, I'm never going to drink." He didn't have a drink in his hand when he said that, but if he had, I would have felt the same way.

That was all that I needed to hear. I shot right-handed, but if he had asked me to play left-handed, I would have done that. If he told me I needed to abstain from drinking to be an NHL player, then that's what I was going to do. I believed my dad always wanted what was best for me. He wouldn't have asked me not to drink unless he felt it would make life better for me.

My dad had the biggest influence on me playing hockey. From the time I was very young, I did everything with my dad. He taught me how to play hockey and baseball.

Everything I am today, and everything I accomplished in the NHL, is because of him. I like to think I'm like my dad. I think I am a great athlete and a great hunter, just like he was. We both had a quiet side. He would never dress like me, but I like to think he was proud that I could pull off my flashy style. Of course, he would never tell me that.

Only once did I hear my dad say, "I love you," and that was to my sister. But you always knew that he loved you. That's all that matters to me.

I was five years old when I started to play minor hockey. I'll never forget my first game. They handed out jerseys, and I went, "Oh my God, I got No. 9!"

I went running out to show my mum and dad. I don't know what it was about No. 9, but that was just my number. And it stuck for my entire career. What's great for me is I did it with my dad. My dad coached me, and he was one of the best coaches I ever had even all the way through the pros. He was hard on me because he knew what I could do. And I mean that in a good way. He wouldn't be hard the same way on one or any of the other kids. He was tough as a coach, and I was lucky to have him teach me. He taught me everything about the game.

My dad could be intimidating. He probably coached two or three of my pee-wee teams. And he played the hell out of me. But I was the best player, so you're going to get that kind of treatment and expect it. When the coach is your dad, you talk about everything. He'd tell me what I did right and what I did wrong. I knew he wasn't going to pat me on the butt very much. You pretty much only get a "Great job tonight" every once in a while. But he didn't have to say that to me. I knew.

Everyone coaches in different ways. Everybody motivates in different ways. With my dad, I always knew what he was trying to tell me. We were on the same page. And that was great.

It was either one of my principals or a teacher in school—I can't remember for sure—who pulled me aside and said, "You've got to pay attention and bear down in school for your future. You can't play hockey all of your life."

"No, you're wrong," I said. "I'm going to play in the NHL."

Everybody who knew me knew that all I thought about was playing hockey. That's all I did.

I remember in Grade 8 having a history teacher named Gerald Irish. And I was terrible in school. I didn't learn until years later that I'm dyslexic. So, I struggled. We had a history test one day after I had a playoff game the night before. And there's no chance that I had studied.

I was sitting back there, and Mr. Irish just slipped me a piece of paper. They were the answers to the test. I had no shot otherwise.

I've had different people ask me if I didn't play hockey, what would I do? Honestly, I can't imagine what I would have done. And I tell people that.

When I was 16 years old, I worked a job where we'd lay blocks. I had to mix the cement and carry blocks to two guys. They would put the blocks in place. I just kept bringing them blocks with cement. I did that for one summer. And after that I said to myself that I'd never work another day in my life. I promised myself that because it was so hard.

In my opinion, I didn't work. Instead, I played a game my whole life. And that's all I've ever known.

I never got to play hockey with my dad. But I did play fast-pitch softball with him. When one of his teammates didn't show up, I would be invited to play. Even at 15, playing against men, I boasted a good glove and hit the ball hard. I played second base and my dad was on first. Even though I played in the NHL, I still list playing on a team with my dad as one of the highlights of my life. At one tournament we played together, I was named the Most Valuable Player. The reward was a watch that had the Labatt's logo on the face. I gave it to my dad.

My dad coached me in both hockey and baseball. A truck driver by trade, he hauled sand and gravel in his own truck. But that work was seasonal. In the winter, he had time to teach his children how to play hockey. He was hard on me, but not on the other kids. He wouldn't be hard on someone who didn't have the skill or ability. He was hard on me in a good way. My dad understood what I could do, and he pushed me to use all of my ability. He made sure I knew how to win faceoffs, block shots, and kill a penalty, as well as score goals. What I learned from him still drives me today. When you are hard on people, some fold right up. Others, when you are hard on them, they go and get things done.

That's the way I was. My dad knew if he gave me a nudge, I could do great things. I always knew that what he wanted me to do was best for me. I trusted that he always had my best interest at heart. I was also confident enough to know that I could do everything he asked me to do.

He was always teaching me, sometimes in unique ways and places. I always say he was the best coach I ever had. My dad understood the game at a different level.

General manager and coach Jimmy Morrison cut me in my first season with Kingston Canadians.

He had already signed some players, including Justin Hanley, a center from Peterborough who was drafted in the second round.

My dad had watched the tryout and went to see Morrison.

"You're making a mistake here," Dad said. "You're taking the wrong player."

That's all he said. He didn't yell and scream. But he wanted Morrison to know that he had missed on his evaluation. My dad knew I should have been picked ahead of Hanley.

Of course, my dad was correct. In 1978–79, I played for North York Rangers and netted 40 goals and totaled 102 points in 50 games. Meanwhile, Hanley scored four goals in 41 games for Kingston. I was called up for two games and had one point.

He'd take me everywhere to play, and I loved it. My dad was a good hockey player, but he never talked about it. We knew very little other than he had a tryout for the Toronto Marlies when he was 13. My first cousin, Craig Stamp, says he played in Cleveland for a time when he was 18 or 19.

My dad grew up in Bobcaygeon, Ontario, 75 kilometers or 45 miles south of West Guilford. He had two brothers and uncles who were players, too.

My dad treated all us kids the same, introducing each of us to the game. For some reason, my interest in the sport was deeper. I just took off. I just couldn't get enough of it. You couldn't keep me away from the rink. We didn't grow up on a farm like my mum did. So, for us, there were no chores. We'd literally be at that rink all day, every day.

The only time I wouldn't be at the rink would be if I was trapping with my dad or at our hunting camp. The Nicholls family has owned and operated a hunting camp since 1960.

We lease 3,700 acres of land and host a two-week deer hunting camp in November, one week of moose hunting in October, and one week of bear hunting in September. The family also duck hunts on the property. Our family has been leasing the land for 61 years. My mum did the cooking.

I probably have as many hunting stories as NHL tales. Again, my dad is front and center in my memories.

My dad was the best shot I ever saw. When I was a kid, I remember him bringing down three ducks with his Model 12 shotgun in a span of five seconds. We were sitting, hiding on a beaver dam. The first duck was flying right at him and the second one was over his head and the third he brought down, leaning back and firing.

Shooting ducks is difficult. You have to lead a duck. Many hunters don't know how to shoot ducks. But my dad knew how to hunt them. Sometimes you have to lead them two or three feet.

We'd go out on a duck hunt, and I would be missing them left and right. It didn't bother me one bit because I was able to watch my dad bring down duck after duck. I loved watching great NHL players because they were so much better than everyone else. That's what it was like to watch my dad when he was duck hunting. He was like the Wayne Gretzky of that sport. He'd always come back with his limit of ducks.

Another time we were hunting moose near Ten Mile Lake in Quebec. It was late; daylight had faded when I saw a moose. I was alone, five or six miles up the lake, when I shot it.

By the time I talked to my dad, it was nightfall. When I called the moose, it came toward me. After I shot it, the moose headed for the lake. I shot it in the neck, and it fell into the lake.

I told Dad the story of the kill and he was just relieved it hadn't run 500 yards into the bush before it died.

"But now what do I do?" I asked.

"Tie the rope to his antlers and drag him down the lake with the boat," Dad said. "The moose will float."

I laughed, but I knew that was exactly what I was going to do. It took me 40 minutes to drag that moose up the lake with my aluminum boat with its small engine. I couldn't go very fast. Because I couldn't see very well, I ran into a couple of sandbars.

My two brothers, Red and David, and my dad could hear me coming the whole time. It was so quiet, and they could hear the engine grinding along. They were standing there laughing as I coasted in. The owner of the lodge had driven his tractor down by the shore, and it pulled the moose out of the water.

Dad didn't say anything, but I could tell he was excited for me. I always knew what he was thinking. My dad was such a knowledgeable hunter, and always knew what to do in every situation you might come across.

Dad had his own rules for what was fair and honorable. That came up one time when a doctor landed his small seaplane on the lake bordering our hunting area. The doctor had spotted a moose from the air, landed, walked a bit, shot the moose, and then spent the night quartering it.

The hunters at our camp had heard the plane. Then they heard a shot, and they weren't sure who was doing the shooting. Our people were all accounted for.

My dad knew no one should be out there, but someone had fired a gun. When our hunters ran into the doctor and his friend the next morning, my brother David and cousin Derrell raised my dad on the walkie-talkie.

Dad showed up and the doctor tried to talk himself out of the trouble he was in. He already had most of the moose stuffed into his plane.

"We'll give you half the moose," the doctor said.

"No, you aren't going to get anything," Dad said. "You pull the moose out of your plane and get out of here."

My dad was a big man, and he could get your attention if he wanted to. You can imagine what the doctor thought seeing my dad, speaking firmly, with the shotgun cradled in his arms.

It's unlikely that the doctor had a moose tag, and he could have gotten into all kinds of trouble had my dad turned him in. The doctor had killed that moose on a Sunday and back then you couldn't hunt on a Sunday. He unloaded the moose from the seaplane and went on his way, probably miffed that he lost his moose meat and thankful that he didn't get into trouble.

Dad and I bonded as much in the great outdoors as we did on the ice or on a ballfield. I shared his love of trapping and hunting, just being outside and enjoying the land. I learned so much just by watching him and trying to please him.

I remember I was about five years old when my dad started teaching me how to trap. Trapping was an important revenue source for the family because local truck drivers didn't work much, if at all, during the winter months.

When I was young, I remember Dad skinning a muskrat in less than a minute. It was unbelievable. He had skinned so many that he had become an expert. It would take me three or four minutes to do a muskrat. A beaver's probably 20 minutes.

Most people won't eat a muskrat, but we did. We would have a muskrat fry.

You cut the spine and the back legs. You take the front legs off. So it's just the back, the back legs. A muskrat is all meat on bone. It just peels right off. My dad loved muskrat, and all the kids did, too. If you think about muskrat, it lives in the water and eats grass and fruits. It's the cleanest animal there is.

You can eat beaver, too. You can eat the hindquarter of a beaver. It was never as good. But muskrats were as good as it gets.

Back in the day, when the prices were good, you'd earn $100 or $125 for a beaver pelt, $125 for a muskrat, and $150 for an otter. If you trapped a fisher, you might get $200 or more. My dad would always give me money, and I mean a lot of money for a 10-year-old, when I trapped for him.

I know the money my parents had for Christmas was from his trapping. He always did his trapping before the ice covered the lakes and rivers.

One time, my dad was at the hunting camp, and I was staying with my aunt and uncle because I had to go to school. I was nine or 10 years old, and I was trapping down the river. I remember catching a couple raccoons and some other animals. I had to shoot them because they were still alive. I took them home, we'd go into the camp, and I'd give them to my dad. They'd drive me in after school. I'd give them to him, and he'd always skin them and give me money for them. Maybe that's why I gave it to him later. I remember him giving me $200 to $300 when I was 10 or 11 years old.

Dad taught me to shoot when I was 10. It was like being taught chess by a grand master. I still remember going target shooting when I was that young. You'd have eight or 10 people put a dollar into the pot and then you would shoot at the targets. The closest to the center won the turkey.

My dad taught me so much about hunting and hockey. I shot some squirrels when I was young, but you can't get your license to truly hunt until you're 15.

After I retired from the NHL, I would still trap with my dad. He was older and it was harder for him to set the traps. He would sit in the truck and wait for me while I paddled out in a canoe and set our traps. I would do it to help him and also because I liked being with him. It was fun for me.

When he got older, his hands weren't as strong. I did most of the skinning. He'd try to give me money and I would never take it. He still used trapping money to get him through the winter.

I was always impressed that Dad remembered, with details, every beaver house he had ever come across. Even if he had trapped at a beaver house 15 years before, he would remember where the doors were located.

That's how you trap the animals. You set traps at the places where they come in and out of their home.

Sometimes I could walk to the beaver dam, but we also had a canoe in the truck, and I would use that to reach them.

One year I brought my girlfriend Jun Lee back to West Guilford. She was a pro golfer from San Jose who loved the outdoors. But she didn't love it when we struck a log and flipped our canoe on our way to a beaver house. It was November and the water was freezing.

Trapping comes with some danger. When my dad was almost 60, he flipped a canoe and went completely under water while setting traps. It has happened to every trapper. But it happened to Dad at the worst time. He could swim. But the water was frigid. It was January. Soaking wet in freezing temperatures, he had to climb back into the canoe, make his way back to shore, place the canoe in his truck, and drive home.

When I called home that day, my mum told me the story. Because he was okay, we laughed about it. He ended up with pneumonia. But it could have been a far worse situation.

In the fall of 2013, we were at our hunting camp and Dad had a debilitating upset stomach. He couldn't hunt that morning. He stayed in bed. I had never seen him do that.

We knew something was wrong and we convinced him to see a doctor. He came out, sat on the porch, and then said he was ready to get in the truck. I helped him into the truck. As I moved his leg into the cab, his head went down, and his mouth closed. I believe he died right there. But we weren't sure. We were a long way from the hospital. My mother and sister jumped in, and I raced off to meet the ambulance. He was transported to the hospital, but it was already too late.

Even today it's still difficult for me to talk about this. Doctors weren't sure exactly how he died. He had been on oxygen for a while. Our generator allowed him to still come to the camp. To me, it seemed like a heart attack. But doctors believed it was probably an aneurysm that burst.

All I can add is that I am thankful that I was with him when he died. I am thankful my dad was at our hunting camp when this happened because there was no place he'd rather be on any given day.

Many people came to the funeral home, and everyone had a story about him. I stood by the casket and greeted people. The line never stopped. People came that we didn't know. But he had helped them, or they had met him along the way. I wanted to be a pallbearer. I wanted to be the one who lowered him into the ground. But I didn't give a eulogy. I could not have done it. My uncle and cousin gave the eulogy. My dad would have understood. I am like him. We couldn't, or wouldn't, speak about how we felt. But we both knew how we felt about each other.

We buried my dad wearing the Labatt's watch I had given him.

Still, to this day, there is nothing I like more than talking about my dad. It's been eight years since he passed but I still feel his loss.

I was always less inclined to get myself into trouble if I was around my dad.

A few years after Dad passed away, I hunted another massive buck for five consecutive days near the end of our hunting season. I'd go out at dark and hunt until 11:00 AM. I would also go out in the afternoon and hunt for a while. It was December. It was -24 degrees Celsius (-11 Fahrenheit). I had him coming in a couple of times, but the shot was never right. The deer season ended on December 15, and I missed it because I was involved in charity hockey events.

But my dad wasn't there to tell me not to hunt out of season. I went out and hunted that deer for two more days. There were plenty of deer in the area, and on the second night I saw them all scatter from behind me. I turned around and saw a game warden walking toward me. There was nowhere to hide.

He escorted me back to my truck and read me my rights. He seized my $1,000 bow and all my arrows. Those weren't going to be returned to me. You either get a court date or you can pay the prescribed fine. You also lose your hunting license.

I negotiated with the prosecutor for two years probation instead of a lost license. Hunting was too important to me. Because I kept my license, my fine doubled to $5,000. It was a costly lesson.

And I knew when the game warden was walking me back to the truck that I never would have hunted illegally if Dad was still around. I miss him every day.

I survived 1,245 NHL games counting the playoffs. And then I almost was done in by an angry moose.

I had my share of NHL injuries. But I never had a scary moment in hockey like I had when a moose charged me in Jackson Hole, Wyoming.

The 700-pound moose actually charged me twice.

I was in Jackson Hole for an annual hockey event. I wasn't hunting. In fact, I had gone out for a drive hoping to take some photographs of animals. I spotted a moose lying down by the river. As I walked down toward the moose for a closer shot, she spotted me and started to walk away.

Then, without warning, she turned and charged me. It was like the moose thought, *Fuck you, I'm going after that guy.*

I was about 30 yards when she started her charge. I had nowhere to go. I braced myself, like I would if I was going to be run over by a 230-pound defenseman. At the last second, the moose spun around and the snow from its hooves sprayed me.

It was like in a hockey game when a player comes to a quick stop and the ice chips spray into the goalie's face.

She turned away, and I started to leave. The guy I was with started yelling at me and the moose turned back and came at me again. I thought for sure she would run me over. I knew this was a dangerous situation. People don't realize that moose kill more people than grizzly bears over the course of a year.

A moose will paw the hell out of you and stomp on you and kick you. I thought this moose was going to bulldoze me. All she did was scare the hell out of me a second time.

Not sure to this day why she came after me. Maybe she was pregnant. It was March.

Since my retirement, my interest in hunting has grown. Because my dad died at our hunting camp, people think it might be sad for me to go to that camp. But it's not sad at all. My dad was happiest when he was at that camp.

When my dad died, he was where he would have wanted to be. Some of our best moments together as a family came at that camp.

My dad knew every inch of that land. When I was younger, I would go out alone and lose my bearings in the vastness of the 3,500 acres. It's not hard to do. I'd use a walkie-talkie to reach my dad.

He'd ask me to describe the landscape around me. I'd talk to him about the size of rocks, clumps of trees, and what I could see in the distance.

"I know where you are at," he'd say.

He would drive out in that general direction and then say, "Just follow the sound of my horn."

Of course, Dad would be right about where I was and I would be back with him in a matter of minutes.

No one enjoyed hunting more than my dad. There are many expert hunters out there, but no one was better than my dad. He knew everything about hunting, and no one was better with a shotgun. I believe if my dad was given a chance to come back to life for one day, he would spend it duck hunting.

Anything that happened great in my life, my dad was the first person I wanted to tell. Wherever I went after my retirement, I always took my dad. There was not anyone I was closer to than my dad.

When I was playing, I liked to do things for my parents because they meant so much to me.

When I was playing in New Jersey, I went gambling with Devils teammate Claude Lemieux right before we left on a road trip that started in Toronto.

I had a good night and walked away from Atlantic City with an envelope containing $10,000 in cash.

The envelope came with me to Toronto. When I went up to my parents' hotel room in Toronto, I handed my dad the envelope. He was shocked. I don't have any idea what he used it for, probably to pay bills. I gave it to him because I knew they could use the money. It was up to him how he chose to spend it. My dad always had to work hard to make ends meet.

He was a remarkable person. If he was driving down the road and saw someone stranded on the road, he would always stop to help. He never said much, but he cared about people.

Maybe he cared too much. I bought public storage units in our hometown, and he ran them. After he died, we realized he was too nice of a guy. He wasn't a businessman.

He didn't charge nearly enough for our storage units. They were paying next to nothing. It was like he would charge people what they could afford to pay. People would pay when they could. He didn't have anyone's phone number or basic information. He really didn't do much record keeping.

When I took control of the place, I realized we had no idea who was renting each of our units. We didn't know if they were paid up or behind on their rent.

We had one customer who had been using our facility for seven years and had never paid a cent. He knew her and she probably needed a break. I'm sure he never even brought it up to her that she owed rent for her storage unit. That was my dad. If someone said he or she couldn't afford to pay, my dad would say, "Okay."

I believe the woman who didn't pay for seven years ended up giving us a couple of months' rent.

After we took over, I was forced to double the rent fees just to make the business viable.

That's just who he was as a person, and I loved him for that.

At our hunting facility, there's a photo of me, my dad, and my brothers with the Stanley Cup hanging on the wall by the door. It gives me joy to see it there. There's another photo of him with a deer by the door. We see my dad each time we go out hunting. It doesn't make me sad to be at that camp. I think about all the good times we had there.

Recently, I was driving into our hunting camp with my girlfriend. One of my dad's favorite Merle Haggard songs popped up on the radio. I told my girlfriend that was no coincidence.

"There is Dad saying hi and telling me he's glad I'm here," I told her.

CHAPTER 22

SCORING GOALS, HUNTING MOOSE

BRYAN WATSON PLAYED 16 YEARS in the NHL by being the league's most annoying player. His nickname was "Bugsy" because he was a super pest, a player who could get under a player's skin while checking him nonstop.

The Watson legend was born during the 1966 playoffs when the Detroit Red Wings, weary of being beaten by Bobby Hull's offensive might, assigned the 165-pound Watson to check the 195-pound Hull. Watson pushed Hull to the edge with his irritating presence and physical play. Hull only scored two goals in six games and the Red Wings won the series. Hull refused to discuss Watson with the media. But everyone else in the league was talking about him.

Bugsy was from Bancroft, Ontario, a 45-minute drive from Haliburton. Every hockey person in my area knew who he was, and I ran into him the summer of 1981, a couple of months before my first Los Angeles Kings training camp. I ran into him while working at the hockey school in Haliburton. He had some advice for me that I've never forgotten.

"First thing you've got to do at training camp? Take your stick and whack someone right over the head," Bugsy said. "Punch 'em! Do something to get the coach's attention. You've got to go win your job!"

I was laughing hard when Bugsy was telling me this, but he was trying to make a serious point. He was a little crazy, but in a good way.

What he lacked in skill he more than made up with his tenacity and willingness to do whatever it took to be successful. That's why he was able to survive all those years, playing with the Montreal Canadiens, Oakland Seals, Detroit Red Wings, Pittsburgh Penguins, St. Louis Blues, and Washington Capitals, plus the World Hockey League's Cincinnati Stingers. He played until he was 36. Bugsy had only retired two seasons before he gave that advice.

Sadly, he died while we were writing this book. But I remember his advice because he was right in his own way. I didn't hit anyone over the head with my stick in my first training camp, but I heard what he said, and I tried to make sure coaches noticed me for standing up for myself and hitting some people.

I was going to make my living as a scorer, but I wanted to make sure everyone knew I would stand up for myself and wasn't shy about throwing hits.

One of my favorite quotes that came out of this book-writing process came from Darryl Sutter. When he was asked about what kind of player I was, he said, "What gets overlooked in his career—being unique with his personality and his style of play—is that he was a great competitor and didn't take any shit from anybody. And he expected his teammates to be the same way."

Sutter might have known my game as much or maybe better than any coach I ever had. He showed trust in me when I was in Chicago and in San Jose with him.

One problem I had as an NHL player, particularly when I was young, was that I enjoyed playing the game so much that I was often seen with a smile on my face even on the ice. General managers would see me laughing on the ice about something and see that as an indication that I didn't care, or I wasn't serious about the game.

The best argument I have against that notion is Darryl Sutter. Do you think that Darryl Sutter would have wanted me around if he thought for even a second that I didn't care about winning?

The answer is no.

Darryl may not have appreciated how I lived my life, but he knew I gave it all that I had when I was playing an NHL game.

People have always asked me what I'm most proud about from my NHL career and I always say, "Just that I made the fucking NHL."

I was gratified that some of my former teammates said they had a completely different perception about what kind of player I was after they played on the same team with me.

What some in the hockey world didn't seem to understand is that I was serious all the time about competing and trying to win. But I was just having fun while I was doing it. I was getting paid incredibly well to play a game I loved. Why shouldn't I be happy about that?

I'm still in touch with my inner kid. I always try to have fun at whatever I'm doing. I shouldn't have to apologize that I enjoyed everything about being an NHL player.

Just because I like to prank my teammates and wear a fur coat to the game doesn't mean I don't want to win. As a matter of fact, I hate losing. I'm a bad loser.

But I would bet that there is a percentage of players, coaches, and general managers from my era who would describe me as too fun-loving for my own good.

I scored 475 goals over my career, and I'm only one of eight players to score 70 or more goals in a season. I must have done something right. But I think everyone who played with me understood that I cared deeply about my teams.

When we were finishing up this book, I was still 53rd on the all-time scoring list. A lot of fucking guys have played in the NHL. Being 53rd is an accomplishment.

Some amazingly talented guys are right around me on that list, including some Hall of Famers. Lanny McDonald finished with 500 goals. Darryl Sittler had 484. Sergei Fedorov is at 483. Denis Savard finished at 473. Pat LaFontaine has 468.

I actually ended up with more points than Sittler. He finished with 1,121 and I totaled 1,209.

I don't have any regrets about my career. As I previously mentioned, I wish I would have won a Stanley Cup as a player. Winning one as a Los Angeles Kings power play consultant was fun, but I'm confident winning one as a player would be far more rewarding.

Also, I wish I could have played more than 126 games as Wayne Gretzky's teammate. I had 97 goals in those 126 games. Being the No. 2 center when Gretzky is the No. 1 center has its advantages, especially if you also get some power play time with the Great One.

I was 29, in the prime of my career, when the Kings traded me to the New York Rangers in 1990. Wayne played six more seasons in Los Angeles. Had I not been traded, and stayed with Wayne, I would have probably averaged 30 to 40 goals per season. I might have ended up with more than 600 goals.

Even though I fell short of earning membership in the NHL's 500-goal club, I always felt like I was one of the NHL's top scorers. In my nine years in Los Angeles, I averaged 39 goals per season. In my one complete season with the Rangers, I posted 73 points in 71 games. Only Brian Leetch had more points than me. I was a point-per-game player (49 points in 49 games) in my first Oilers season and was the team's leading scorer when I was traded to the Devils. In New Jersey, I was among the leading scorers in terms of points per game. I averaged 20 goals per season in Chicago, even though I missed a bunch of games with injuries.

At 35, I signed with San Jose and was third in scoring in my first season there.

It's hard to explain why I was able to create offense no matter who I played with or how good our team was. My dad certainly taught me some tricks to help in the offensive zone. But I've always felt that scoring was a gift. A small number of players received that gift. Most didn't.

From the time I was seven or eight years old, I could see the game differently than most players. I didn't hope I would score. I expected I would score. My confidence grew considerably in junior, particularly in my last season when I scored 63 goals and 152 points in 65 games to lead the team. Scott Howson was second on Kingston with 57 goals and 110 points. It was a wild scoring race that Ontario Hockey League season. I finished third behind John Goodwin of Sault Ste. Marie (56+110=166) and Windsor's Ernie Godden (87+66=153).

Godden played only five games in the NHL with Toronto in 1981–82 and Goodwin played only in the minors. I hit Goodwin once in the corner. He was small, maybe 135 pounds, about the same size as my adult daughter. He could get away with being small in junior. I was third in the scoring race, and five of the next top seven scorers all played in the NHL (Tony Tanti, Steve Ludzik, Howson, Steve Larmer, and Randy Cunneyworth).

Other than Scotty, whose NHL career was 18 games with the Islanders, I don't remember who I played with in Kingston. We had a great power play because we had such good defense. Rik Wilson and Neil Belland were our next highest scorers. Wilson had 70 assists and 100 points. Belland totaled 28 goals and 82 points.

When I got to Los Angeles, I just thought I would keep scoring. And I did.

When people ask me which goalie gave me the most trouble, my answer is "None of them."

You don't score 475 goals in the NHL if you allow goalies to get inside your head. Scoring came easy to me. You never want to say that in a cocky way. But scoring came naturally to me. I didn't think about it. I just did it and I enjoyed it. I like to see players get excited when they score. I appreciate that Alex Ovechkin uncorks a celebration when he finds the back of the net. It's tough to score a goal against NHL competition. Coaches spend hours upon hours scheming to prevent you from scoring. You should celebrate when you score.

I loved playing the game, and I let it show. People might have labeled me as a character, that I was flamboyant, or it looked like I was having too much fun. I played the game with a smile on my face. And not all my coaches liked it, no doubt. Ask anyone who played with me. I was extremely competitive, and I only wanted to win. Ever since I was a kid I got excited when I scored, and I showed it.

I had a way of celebrating goals that started when I was young, and I did it in the NHL, too. Bob Miller, the great Kings announcer, named it the "Pumper Nicholl."

After I scored, I'd hold my stick in my left hand and I'd raise my right knee almost to my waist. I'd rock back and pump my right arm either up and down or windmill it while I skated down the ice. The bigger the goal the more I'd celebrate.

I did it in every city I played. And I did it when I arrived in Los Angeles in 1981–82. It didn't matter that not many NHLers were celebrating their goals with the same enthusiasm I had after scoring. I had to be me.

The nickname "Pumper Nicholl" stuck. It really stuck. Here it is 40 years later, and people ask me to sign autographs with "Pumper Nicholl." I guess that's how they choose to remember me. I've had a number of women ask me to sign "Pumper Nicholl" on different body parts.

When you play in the NHL you should want to share your career with your friends, family, and fans. That's what it is all about.

I always wanted to think that I was playing for me and my dad. He had helped me grow into a pro player and I wanted him to share in my career as much as he could.

My mum never missed one of my games on television once I got them a satellite hook-up. I wanted my siblings to share in my success, to have some enjoyment from what I was doing.

My brother, David, tells a story, with some fondness, about the family getting together to listen to my game on the radio when I played in Kingston.

"It was almost like the old Foster Hewitt days," David said. "We were gathered as a family at home around our old stereo, and my dad had the game on the radio. Bernie scored a fairly significant goal in the playoffs. He was playing with and against a lot of good players. That's when I thought to myself, 'well,' as they say, 'maybe there's a chance!'"

Erin was nine years younger than me. "Right from the get-go I was watching him when he left home," Erin said. "He made a huge impression and made me want to play hockey for sure. Bernie was always good about letting us in the locker room to meet the guys."

I have many mementos from my playing days, but I have even more memories about the joy that was spread around by my NHL career. When my teams would play in Toronto, my parents would get five or six hotel rooms to bring their friends to see me play.

Because they knew my parents, people ended up feeling like they had an inside connection to the NHL. Isn't that what sports should be about? I think we can say that throughout my career I never lost sight of the truth that sports are supposed to be an entertaining endeavor for everyone involved.

I respect that the game is big business. But that doesn't mean we can't enjoy ourselves playing it.

I loved when I could bring smiles to people by just making their experience enjoyable. Isn't that what we are supposed to do in this job? Aren't we entertainers?

My parents would come whenever I would be within driving distances. They came to Buffalo a few times and made it to Chicago when I was there.

Today, NHL teams have dad trips and mom trips. It would have been nice if they had those back when I played. I can imagine that Pat Quinn would have loved my dad and vice versa.

When it comes to the variety of my NHL experiences, I hit the jackpot. I played in Los Angeles; I played alongside Wayne Gretzky. I played for Bruce McNall, who was more like a friend than the owner of the team. I don't know how many times I was in McNall's office just talking about everything and anything.

For a man who amassed enough wealth to buy the Los Angeles Kings, Bruce was really a down-to-earth guy. He was generous to a fault and always looking to have some fun. That's my kind of guy. Lucky outcomes always seemed to happen for Bruce. I'm really surprised he didn't win a Cup with Gretzky.

I played for two Original Six teams (New York Rangers and Chicago Blackhawks), I was traded for Mark Messier, and I played for a Canadian team (Edmonton Oilers).

All that I missed out on was winning the Stanley Cup as a player. But at least I contributed to a championship team as a consultant to coach Darryl Sutter. I was on the ice during the Kings' celebration and received my 24 hours with the Stanley Cup.

I've kept busy in retirement. I haven't worked in a real job. All my hunting is done with a bow these days. There's something more exhilarating about hunting with a bow. The first bull I ever brought down was eight yards away when I shot him.

Another one of my goals is to land a grizzly with a bow. Even though more hunters are killed by moose than bears, there is some fear in bear hunting.

When we hunt bears at our camp, you sometimes end up alone waiting for bears to show themselves after darkness falls.

That's when we start seeing hunters making their way back to our camp.

It's really a great time to hunt, but they say, "Nothing going on out there tonight."

It feels safer sitting in the bunkhouse playing cards than waiting in the dark for a bear.

I have brought down 15 moose with a gun and eight with a bow. The biggest moose I've landed had a 59-inch antler rack.

My goal is to bring down a moose with a 70-inch rack. I'd settle for 66 inches, but a 70-inch moose would be the ultimate for me.

I'm planning a trip next year to the Yukon, up near Dawson, to take a shot at achieving that objective. If you bag a 70-inch moose, that's like scoring 70 goals in an NHL season.

If I can get that moose, I'm pretty sure I would be the only person in the world to score 70 goals in an NHL season and hang a 70-inch moose rack in the house.

Acknowledgments

PEOPLE OFTEN SAY YOU ARE A PRODUCT of your upbringing and surroundings. I can honestly say I am proud to be a small-town guy with traditional values. I would like to thank my mom and dad for instilling this in me. You both were always my biggest supporters and my biggest critics, which kept me grounded and proud of my roots.

We never thank our family enough. I would be half the man I am today without the love and guidance of my sisters, Alberta and Cheryl, and my brothers, Dave and Erin. I always want you to be proud of me because I am certainly proud of all of you. I am not one who would say much to my family, but I want you all to know that I am the luckiest brother in the world knowing you are all behind me.

The greatest day of my life was when I became a father with the birth of my twins, McKenna and Flynn. I am truly blessed to have two beautiful adult children that continue to make me proud. Another blessing came my way on August 11, 2020, with the birth of my first grandson, Rhett. Grandpa loves you so much!

My hockey journey had many twists and turns. I would like to thank my agents Rick Curran and Mike Barnett for your guidance and respect. A big thank you to my cousin Craig Stamp and his wife, Sherrie, for allowing me to live with them while I played Junior B for Woodstock.

If it wasn't for Craig persuading my dad to let his 16-year-old son leave home, my story would have had a different outcome. A warm thank you to my Junior A billets in Kingston, Vern and Sylvia Walters, who gave me a home away from home. Your kindness will never be forgotten. Thank you to all my coaches and trainers from minor hockey all the way through to the pros, especially Ray Tufts, Pete Demers, Ken Lowe, and Dave Smith.

A special thank you to Bruce McNall, who made my time in Los Angeles special. You cared for all your players and still are the most generous man I have ever met. Thank you to Darryl Sutter for giving me the opportunity to be a part of your Stanley Cup winning coaching staff in Los Angeles. Your faith in me during such a historic championship gave me the confidence I needed to pursue my future endeavors. Finally, holding the Stanley Cup over my head and taking it back to my hometown of West Guilford, I will forever be indebted. While in Los Angeles, I was lucky enough to be introduced to many celebrities. Thank you, Tom Hanks, for showing me what "real class" looks like, and how to be kind to others.

Thank you for putting me on the map by wearing my Rangers jersey on *Saturday Night Live*. All of Canada knew who I was that night. Thank you for your continued friendship. Life is nothing without good friends, and I have many. Thank you to all my aunts and uncles, cousins, and hometown buddies who supported me throughout my entire career. Special thanks to Bernie, Michael, Derrell, and Wade.

To my Vegas friends, thanks to the Meeks boys, Chief, Aaron, and Eric. I was blessed to have played with and against arguably some of the greatest players our sport will ever see. I cannot thank you all but would like to shout out to a few who have changed my life for the better.

Thank you Gretz for giving me some of my greatest memories and moments in my hockey career. You treated me with respect and your generosity and friendship I will cherish forever. You showed me how to be a pro and the importance of work ethic that I have carried forward in my life after hockey. Thank you, Mario, for allowing me to have a front-row seat watching you perform your magic during my entire career. You have always treated me with respect on and off the ice and pushed me to be better. Your invites to your golf tournaments and fantasy camps post NHL have inspired me to start my own charitable foundation. Your devotion and commitment to children in need is admirable and something I aspire to be.

In Chicago, I met Chris Chelios, Gary Suter, and Jeremy Roenick, three of the craziest guys and best friends I know. I have said many times that if I could have played with one player my whole career, I would want it to have been Chris Chelios. I thought I knew what working out was until I met Cheli. Gary was a quiet leader and a workhorse. I loved teeing him up for one-timers. One of the hardest and most accurate shooters ever. J.R. was by far the fiercest competitor I ever played with, and some would say the most controversial.

In my opinion, you are someone who is not afraid to speak your mind and stand up for what you believe in. That is what I love about you, buddy.

Thank you to Gary Leeman, one of my closest friends and golfing buddies. Gary, I am sure with some luck and practice, one day you might beat me. Thank you, Luc Robitaille, the greatest goal scorer I ever played with. You have always been someone I can count on for help and guidance. Thank you, Marty McSorley; together we had many stops along the way. You are a warrior and a player who I have always admired for what you had to do night in and night out. You will never find a greater guy in our game, someone who would give you the shirt off his back, a true friend.

Thank you, Joe Murphy. Murph, you were the greatest roommate a player could ever have. Finally, for everyone who made this book possible: Bill Ames and Michelle Bruton from Triumph Books. Ross McKeon, who guided me through this process. My friend and business partner, Scott Sutherland, and his wife, Carolynn, who encouraged me to tell my story and for all those who were interviewed, I thank you from the bottom of my heart.

—Love you all!
Bernie

How apropos is this? As a newspaper beat reporter covering the San Jose Sharks, I took a fold-up map of Canada into the locker room after a practice during the 1998–99 season and asked players to locate their hometowns since a number hailed from remote outposts and it might make a fun story. After a couple found theirs, Bernie Nicholls scoured the map but couldn't find his listed. Catching grief from all corners of the room, Bernie nonetheless continued to raise his voice with displeasure that West Guilford did not appear. "Hey, if Eagle Lake is on this map, West Guilford should be, too. They're no bigger than us!" Fast forward more than two decades later and imagine my great fortune to not only reunite with Bernie, but also that the very premise of his autobiography centers on the fact he came from a very small town to eventually thrive with a brilliant playing career under the bright lights of the NHL.

I want to thank Triumph Books for the opportunity to help bring Bernie's story to life in print. I echo Bernie's appreciation to his ex-teammates, opponents, management, and ownership while singling out Gary Brohman, Brian Burke, Marcel Dionne, Tie Domi, Jim Fox, Grant Fuhr, Clark Gillies (who sadly passed away recently), Adam Graves, Tony Granato, Claude Lemieux, Bob Miller, Bryan Trottier, Tiger Williams, and Doug Wilson for sharing stories of time spent with Bernie on the ice or away from the rink. My deep appreciation goes to Bernie's immediate family who shared their recollections of life in West Guilford and how they proudly watched Bernie grow into a superstar, keeping his priorities in line, without forgetting where he came from or losing his small-town values. A huge thanks to Wayne Gretzky for his gracious giving of time for this project and his wonderful prose provided for the book's foreword. I second Bernie's take that there's no better ambassador for the game of hockey than the Great One. Special thanks to colleagues, members of broadcast media, and other friends in high places including George Johnson, Jim Matheson, Curtis Pashelka, Rick Sadowski, Mark Soltau, Art Spander, Arthur Thorson, and Dan Wood for their assistance and support. Thanks to web sites hockey-reference.com, hockeyDB.com, and NHL.com to fill in the holes and verify information.

A big thank you to my technologically inclined daughter, Lorelei McKeon, to make the process seamless and efficient. Thanks to her brother, Cameron, and my lovely wife, Nadine, for their patience and understanding for the nights on end I was locked in my office on the phone and in front of the computer. And, most of all, I want to thank Bernard I. Nicholls for his unwavering and engaging cooperation throughout the months of detailing his life's story. Thank you for sharing all the conversations filled with poignant introspection, raw honesty and stories that left many of our FaceTime sessions filled with laughter. He may have come from humble beginnings, but Bernie definitely put West Guilford on the map.

—Ross McKeon

Thanks to Bernie Nicholls, Ross McKeon, and Triumph Books for bringing me into this project late in the game.

I've known Ross for a long time and appreciated the heavy lifting he did creating the framework and material for this work. He is a true professional.

Also want to lay some gratitude and praise on Bernie. I've done several as-told-to books and I can honestly say I've never had a bad experience. I enjoy the genre, athletes, and the process. But my time with Bernie was special. Every time we talked it was like an amusement park ride. Every interview was an entertaining journey with twists, turns and lengthy moments of unfiltered fun.

Bernie is honest, funny, caring, and full of energy. He lives the way he played: all in.

It is clear to me that, even when Bernie was playing in the NHL, he never lost his wide-eyed wonder about playing a game he loved. I hope that's the message that comes through with this book. Even today, he is thankful for his career and that he was able to share his career with parents.

Finally, I want to thank Triumph Books for the relationship I've had with them for 30 years. I've lost track of how many of my books have been published by Triumph. The folks at Triumph have always been easy to work with.

That is certainly true with Jesse Jordan, who was the editor on this project. Thanks, Jesse, for taking care of this project.

—**Kevin Allen**